DRACULA COUNTRY

By the same author

THE UNEXPLAINED
FRONTIERS OF THE UNKNOWN
APPARITIONS AND GHOSTS
A GALLERY OF GHOSTS
RIDDLE OF THE FUTURE

DRACULA COUNTRY

Travels and Folk Beliefs in Romania

ANDREW MACKENZIE

ARTHUR BARKER LIMITED   LONDON
A subsidiary of Weidenfeld (Publishers) Limited

ISBN 0 213 16658 5

Printed in Great Britain by
Bristol Typesetting Co. Ltd,
Barton Manor, St Philips, Bristol.

Contents

Contents

Acknowledgements

I wish to thank the many scholars in Romania who have given their time so willingly to me and in particular Dr Ştefan Pascu, member of the Romanian Academy and Rector of Cluj University, Dr Dumitru Pop, Dean of the Faculty of Philology, Dr Gheorghe Pavelescu and Dr Ioan A. Popa, also of Cluj University; Dr Vasile Drăguţ, Director of the Department of Historic and Art Monuments ; Dr Dan Berindei, Vice-President of the Scientific Council of the Historical Institute (or, more correctly, the Institute of History 'Nicolae Iorga') ; Dr Corneliu Bărbulescu, principal scientific researcher at the Institute for Ethnological and Dialectological Research ; Professor Alexandru Misiuga, Director of the National Tourist Office, Bistriţa-Năsăud, and Professor Ştefan Mosora, Director of the Museum of History at Sighişoara.

I also wish to thank the Ministry of Tourism in Bucharest for arranging the facilities for my research visits and for their sympathetic understanding of the project. In particular I would like to thank Mr Dumitru Gheorghe, Director General of the National Tourist Office, Mr Renato Iliescu, head of the Press Department at the Ministry, Mr Oreste Ungureanu and Mr Ionel Gheorghe, both former Directors of the Romanian Tourist Office in London and now at the Ministry in Bucharest, and also the three excellent interpreters, Mr Aurel Câmpeanu, Mr Nicolae Păduraru and Mr Manuel Simonis.

I wish to thank Messrs Robert Hale for permission to quote from *Dracula* by Dr Radu Florescu and Dr Raymond T. McNally, Mr Gabriel Ronay for permission to quote from his book, *The Dracula Myth,* John Murray for permission to quote from *Raggle-Taggle* by Dr Walter Starkie, Garnstone

Press for permission to quote from *Romanian Invitation* by Mr
William Forwood, The New English Library in England and
Clarkson N. Potter Inc. in America for permission to quote
from *The Annotated Dracula* by Professor Leonard Wolf, and
Souvenir Press for permission to quote from *Sex and the Occult*
by Mr Gordon Wellesley.

Preface

This was originally meant to be a book about folk beliefs in Romania, a country I have visited yearly since 1968, mainly for journalistic purposes, but in the course of writing it I have widened the scope to include other aspects of a country whose history goes back well over 2,000 years, but which is in a political sense very new. Modern Romania, comprising Wallachia, Moldavia and Transylvania, came into existence at the end of the first world war, although the three countries were united briefly under Michael the Brave in 1600. Little has been published in the West about modern Romania and even less about folk beliefs there. I do not know any book in English that deals adequately with the true folk beliefs of the Romanian countryside nor do any of the Romanian scholars I consulted. I trust that this volume will meet that need. I regard myself as extremely fortunate in having been able to talk to some of Romania's leading folklorists in research trips in 1974, 1975 and 1976 and in being able to do field work in mountain villages, where belief in ghosts, witches, werewolves and other animals transformed in shape, the forest maiden, the *zmeu*, a flame that changes into a man, and dragons on which witches ride, still lingers.

'But what about vampires?' a reader will inquire. 'Bram Stoker's *Dracula* is all about vampires, and everyone knows about the vampires in Transylvania.' Indeed they do, judging by the world-wide success of *Dracula*. Although some modern writers, but not specialists in folklore, who have recently visited Transylvania declare that the people there still believe in vampires, I have not found any Romanian scholar who subscribes to this belief nor did any of the old people I interviewed mention vampires. Bodies *were* staked in the grave in old Transylvania, but not apparently to prevent the corpse from becoming a vampire. Vampire stories have always seemed to me to be crude and sensational, more fiction than fact, and in my opinion they lack the charm and strangeness of many of the traditional beliefs of the Romanian countryside. Stories about vampires do enjoy a vogue, and I will discuss some of the reasons for this and the Dracula cult in the following pages. Bram Stoker's Count Dracula is the horror figure who dominates a book that is a best seller of best sellers, but there was also an historical Dracula, a fifteenth-century prince of Wallachia, and in places in my book the paths of the fictional and historical Draculas meet, which, in a sense, is fitting, as Stoker created his vampire count in the image of what he imagined the historical Dracula to be.

I do not claim to be a specialist in folklore, but this is a subject which touches on psychical research at various points, such as in the study of apparitions, and I have been able to make comparisons between Western and Romanian traditional beliefs in ghosts.

Every true traveller in a foreign country steps, in a sense, in the footprints of those who have travelled there before him and, if he is wise, he takes notice of what they have written. The reason I say this is that Romania has changed so much in the past century that the visitor of today, and even young Romanians, can have little conception of what Transylvania was like in the past century and of the lowly status of the Romanian population there: for instance, Mrs Emily Gerard, the English wife of the Austrian commander of the cavalry brigade in Transylvania in 1883, said in *The Land Beyond the Forest* that ' Of pride the Romanian has little idea as yet. He has too long been treated as a degraded and serf-like being'. But she also said that ' It is scarcely hazardous to prophesy that this people have a great future before them, and that a day will come when, other nations having degenerated and spent their strength, these descendants of the ancient Romans, rising phoenix-like from their ashes, will step forward with a whole fund of latent power and virgin material, to rule as masters where formerly they crouched as slaves.'

Not only do the writings of former travellers throw light on the situation in Romania today but they can also illuminate scenes of the distant past which otherwise would remain in shadow. It was not until I read Charles Boner's *Transylvania; Its Products and Its People* that I began to understand the reasons for the tension between Hungarians and Saxons and why the historical Dracula could make with apparent impunity the raids against the Saxon towns in Transylvania. It is obvious to me that Bram Stoker had read Boner's book in the course of his research for *Dracula* and he probably read Jules Verne's *The Castle of the Carpathians,* published a few years before *Dracula,* to get 'local colour'. Jules Verne had travelled in Transylvania but Stoker had not. Verne wrote much about folk beliefs, as did Emily Gerard, but Charles Boner was more concerned with economics and the political background of the country. He impressed me as being a shrewd observer, and, what is most important in a writer, unbiassed. ' Any traveller in Transylvania will discover the difficulty of obtaining correct information on particular questions owing to the influence of nationality and of political feeling,' Boner wrote over one hundred years ago, and, indeed, it is not easy today to get to the root of some problems. All one can do is to persist, and to go back to Transylvania again and again, as I did, until the answers become clearer.

The writers I have mentioned travelled Transylvania in comfort, but the distinguished Irish scholar, Dr Walter Starkie, saw the country the hard way when he wandered through it with his violin in 1929. The result was that delightful book, *Raggle-Taggle.* Transylvania was then in transition, but the number of gipsies he encountered, and his adventures with them, belonged to a vanishing way of life. The late Dr Starkie, who was born in 1894, wrote of the tensions between Hungarians and Romanians, just as Boner described the tensions between Hungarians and the court in Vienna and between Saxons and Hungarians. I am indebted to Dr Starkie for the window he opened on Transylvania and also to two modern American scholars, Dr Radu Florescu and Dr Raymond T. McNally, for their research on the historical Dracula.

Unfortunately, I do not speak or read Romanian, but I had the benefit of three excellent interpreters provided, with a car and driver, by the Ministry of Tourism. Although I took a tape recorder with me, the number of exchanges necessary between three people made this instrument of little use, so that I had to rely on my notebook. Doubtless errors have crept into my book, but I trust that they are more due to misunderstandings than anything else – time and again the interpreter has said, when a scholar has explained how a certain folk belief should be understood, ' It is very difficult to say this in English '. I have had as many as three separate interviews with some folklorists to elucidate points they have made in previous interviews and followed this up with letters from England to make certain that I have not misunderstood them. All I need to add now is that I have not been subjected to censorship in any way nor has my typescript been seen in advance by any Romanian official before going to my publisher. I should add, however, that I asked Dr Corneliu Bărbulescu, of the Institute for Ethnological and Dialectological Research in Bucharest (formerly the Institute of Ethnography and Folklore), for his views on the chapters on ghosts and werewolves, the most important in the book from a folklore point of view, and he was kind enough to say that he appreciated the objectivity of my interpretation of the information from Romanian folk tradition. Since then these chapters have been altered slightly, particularly to include information from the Royal College of Surgeons of England about the human ' tail ', one of the signs by which you may know a ghost, or *strigoi,* in Romania. Bram Stoker, I feel, knew only part of the Romanian traditions of the undead when he wrote *Dracula.*

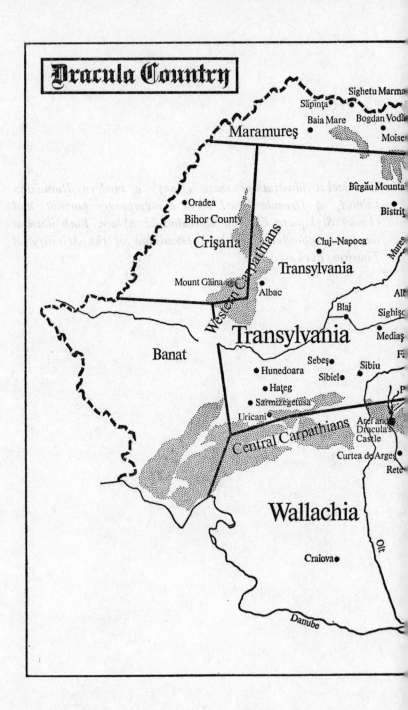

Dracula Country

Sighetu Marma
Săpinţa
Baia Mare
Bogdan Vod
Moise
Maramureş

Bîrgău Mounta
Bistriţ
Oradea
Bihor County
Crişana
Cluj–Napoca
Western Carpathians
Transylvania
Mount Găina
Albac
Mureş
Blaj
Alt
Sighişc
Transylvania
Mediaş
Banat
Fă
Sebeş
Sibiu
Hunedoara
Sibiel
Haţeg
Sărmizegetusa
Uricani
Aref anc
Dracula's
Central Carpathians
Castle
Curtea de Argeş
Rete
Wallachia
Olt
Craiova

Danube

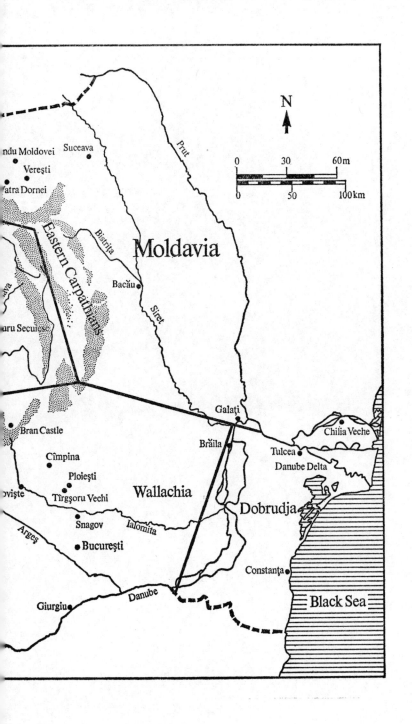

1 The land beyond the forest

My first visit to Transylvania could not have had a more spectacular beginning. A Romanian friend had driven me from the Black Sea to Bucharest, the capital, past the oilfields at Ploieşti, and, as evening approached, we were about to leave the plains for the foothills of the mountains when a violent storm broke out. The sky suddenly darkened, forked lightning illuminated the landscape, hail splattered on the road, a high wind tore up poplars, scattering several on the highway, and across the fields a dust storm swirled, reminding me of a belief held in former days in Transylvania that a whirlwind always denotes that the devil is dancing with a witch, and that whoever approaches too near the dangerous circle may be carried off bodily to hell and sometimes only barely escapes by losing his cap.

Cars were drawn up at the roadside as drivers waited for the storm to slacken in intensity, but the indications were that we were in for a bad night and would have difficulty in reaching Braşov, a medieval city that had been a stronghold of the Saxon settlers, so that we settled for Cîmpina, a small town which is a centre of the engineering industry and of oil refining. The hotel there was full, but we were referred to a private house where travellers unable to find other accommodation were given a bed. We were not the only refugees from the storm. At six o'clock in the morning I drank toasts in brandy with travellers from northern Transylvania, bordering the Soviet Union. We were unable to communicate without an interpreter, but my friend fulfilled that role, and I soon felt the warmth of feeling and sense of hospitality that characterizes the people of Transylvania, a country which, until comparatively recently, has

been a remote part of Europe and even now is too little known:
indeed, some people believe it exists only in horror stories, the
most famous of which is, of course, Bram Stoker's *Dracula*.

How should Dracula country be defined? The novelist C. P.
Snow, in his foreword to William Forwood's *Romanian Invitation* says that the author 'loves every square metre of Romanian
soil, from the Dracula country down to the wild marshes of the
Danube mouths'. I take it that Snow is referring here to fictional
Dracula country, but for the historical figure on whom Stoker
based his novel the Danube Delta *is* Dracula country. A map in
the tower of the ruins of the Prince's Palace at Tîrgovişte, capital
of Wallachia from the fourteenth to the seventeenth century,
shows the Impaler's movements from the Danube Delta (Tulcea)
to Suceava in Moldavia in the north and to Hunedoara in the
west of Romania; to Belgrade, Budapest and the southern bank
of the Danube. It also records that he travelled to Constantinople
as a captive. This watchtower, which may have been built by the
Impaler himself, contains documents, maps, and Dracula's signa-
ture and seal, thus establishing him firmly as an historical personage. As you travel Romania the fictional Count Dracula fades
back into the pages of Stoker's horror story and Vlad the
Impaler, who called himself Dracula or Draculea, takes the stage.
In the West, however, *Dracula,* based on the novel, is still a
popular film or stage play.

Bucharest, the capital, also in Wallachia, is an important part
of Dracula country. The name Bucharest appears for the first
time in a document dated 20 September 1459 during Dracula's
principal reign, so that in a sense he can be called the 'father' of
Bucharest. Archeological excavations have proved that as early as
the fourteenth century there was a strong cluster of villages on
the present territory of Bucharest. It has been maintained that
Dracula built the citadel in Bucharest, but recent restoration
works uncovered a medieval fortification from the second half
of the fourteenth century. This sent the evidence of the existence
of the town one hundred years back to the reign of Mircea the
Old, 1386–1418, Dracula's grandfather and one of the great
figures in Romanian history. But Dracula certainly fortified the

town, and although Tîrgoviște continued to be the capital of
Wallachia during his reign he spent much of his time in
Bucharest. There was a sound military reason for this. Important
trade roads that connected the east with the towns in the west
or with the Russian principalities met in Bucharest, and from
there the commander of the fortress could watch the frontier
along the Danube more closely. The citadel in Bucharest was a
rectangular building of about 800 square metres. All the four sides
were taken up by tall, dark basements covered with roofs made
of thick oak beams. The princely apartments must have been on
the western side. In the middle of the citadel there was an inner
courtyard of about a hundred square metres. It is hard to say
what the ground floor and the higher part of the citadel were
like. The walls uncovered today are only those of the basements,
and were seriously damaged during the successive stages of re-
construction. Bucharest is now a city with a population of
2,000,000 including that of the suburbs.

The Romania of Dracula's day has little connection, in a
political sense, with the Romania of today. There were then two
separate states, Wallachia and Moldavia, both under princes,
or *voivodes,* and the country of Transylvania, which was effec-
tively under Hungarian domination. But confusion will be
avoided if we remember that the population of all three states
was predominantly Romanian and almost entirely so in Moldavia and Wallachia. The Romanians are a very old people,
descendants of the Dacians and Romans, and are therefore a
Latin race. Romania is, in a sense, a Latin island in a Slavonic
sea, if we except the Magyars, and has cultural affiliations with
both East and West.

People have often called Romania the France of eastern
Europe.

Snow writes

Romania is unique. It lies in the heartland of Slavonic Europe,
but it is quite different from the Slav countries – and I can say
that, since I know the Slavs and love them. The Roman legions
left their own Latin language in Romania, the most remote Latin

outpost of the Empire. They left more than that. To this day, Romania not only speaks a language very much like Italian, but has a population which possesses the sparkle, the intelligence, the physical appearance that one meets in Tuscany and the Lombard plain. In the long run they have everything – natural riches, great scenic variety, widespread education, gifted people – which will make for a brilliant future.

Let us now place Romania in its modern framework. Romania has a total area of 91,699 square miles, of which Transylvania comprises 40,685 square miles. The frontiers, extending nearly 2,000 miles, border the Soviet Union in the north and east, Hungary and Yugoslavia in the west, and Bulgaria in the south. Romania is a natural fortress because the Carpathians, a continuation of the Alps, occupy two-thirds of the territory, and within this 'Carpathian redoubt' is Transylvania which, in addition to the mountains, also has a high plateau, bordered by the snowy Făgăraş Mountains. I have been driven along this plateau many times, past the storks in the fields in summer and the many carts drawn by horses with red tassels on their harnesses, reminiscent of the time when this was regarded as protection against the evil eye; the coloured houses in the villages, many with a cross on the walls; the fortified churches situated on high ground for defensive purposes, and the ruins of citadels erected during the Middle Ages to watch over regions swept periodically by invaders. Many of the Saxon churches in particular were strongly built. In the last century it was still possible to find in the Protestant churches a round stone, as large as a cannon ball, hung up by a chain in the porch. Formerly, a girl who had lost her innocence, to use an old-fashioned phrase, was obliged to sit at the church door for a certain number of Sundays with the stone round her neck; and only after thus having expiated her fault was she allowed again to enter the church. For all I know some of these 'penitence stones' may still exist in the churches. When you travel in Romania you invariably brush shoulders with the past. Sometimes it is the past of classical antiquity which you find in the remains of Greek and Roman settlements at the Black Sea. Even in Mamaia, with its complexes of modern hotels, you can be served by a waitress whose features remind you of those of a figure on a Greek vase. A bus ride takes you to Constanţa, the Tomis of antiquity, which, according to legend, was linked in its beginning with a tragic episode in the Argonauts' expedition. The name of the poet Ovid, exiled here in 8 AD by the Emperor Augustus, is a respected one in present day Constanţa. The feeling of the past in Transylvania is entirely different because the Dacians represented another civilization, and foreign influences, Hungarian and Saxon, have intruded.

The last king of the Dacians was Decebal (87–106 AD) who was defeated by the Emperor Trajan. The Dacians, or Getae, who were the northern branch of the Thracians, lived in the numerous villages scattered all over Transylvania. The seat of government was at Sarmizegetusa in the Orăştie Mountains in southern Transylvania. Transylvania has always been rich in silver and gold. The amount of gold taken as booty by Trajan at the end of the second war against the Dacians was so great that it was possible to abolish all taxation in the year 106 and grant a gift of 650 *denarii* to every taxpayer in the Roman Empire. There is a story that before falling on his sword to avoid capture Decebal caused a river to be diverted from its course at great toil and expense. Strong vaulted cellars were constructed in the dry river bed for the storage of gold, silver and precious stones, the whole then being covered with earth and gravel and the river brought back to its original course. The work was carried out by prisoners who were either massacred or deprived of their eyesight to avoid betrayal. Gold coins are still being found in rivers which flow from the Orăştie Mountains, so that there could be some truth in this story, although the possibility that the coins came from individual deposits of buried treasure has to be kept in mind.

Transylvania is today used in a broad sense to designate Romanian territory situated to the west of the Carpathians, that is, the territory lying within the Carpathian arc. Used in this way, says Professor Giurescu in *Transylvania in the History of Romania,* the name designates the province lying between the

bend of the Carpathians and the Apuseni Mountains, or Transylvania proper, the regions of Maramureş, Crişana or the land
of the Criş rivers, and the Banat.

After the withdrawal of the legions by Aurelian in 271 AD
Transylvania was overrun by successive barbaric tribes. The
officials and richer people withdrew across the Danube with the
legions, but the great bulk of the population remained under the
Goths, to whom they paid taxes and tithes. Few documents of
this time exist, but disputes about the continued occupation of
the land by the descendants of the Daco-Romans continue to this
day, although as Professor Giurescu points out in his book,
the Austrian Emperor Joseph II (1765–90) considered the
Romanians to be, in his own words, 'incontestably the oldest and
most numerous inhabitants of Transylvania'. The rich and
fertile country was conquered by the Hungarians in 896–900 AD.
According to Western sources, the Magyars did not fully establish their rule until 1003 AD after the newly crowned King
Stephen had defeated a native prince, Gyula, variously described
as Vlach (Wallach) or Bulgarian by race. Professor Giurescu
says that some historians have tried to demonstrate that the first
Romanians to arrive in the Transylvanian tableland about the
end of the twelfth century were shepherds with their flocks, who
gradually moved northwards, but 'this theory is completely
groundless and is contradicted by the clear and incontestable
documentary evidence at our disposal.'

In order to complete the occupation of Transylvania the
Hungarians colonized the eastern part of the province with
Szeklers, about whom Bram Stoker makes the fictional Dracula
speak with such pride, and Saxons from the Rhineland and
Luxembourg who settled in seven fortified towns. The cautious
Saxons would not come without safeguards, and the chief of
their many privileges was the charter granted to them in 1224
by King Andrew II of Hungary.

By the time Dracula came to the throne of Wallachia the
Saxons had been firmly established in Transylvania for more than
200 years and, in many respects, had acquired a position of
strength which, as a Romanian, he must have bitterly resented.

There were also tensions between the Saxons and the Hungarians. All too often the Hungarian landlords, with their great estates, were absentee landlords, and the Romanian majority were treated as an inferior race. As Dr Starkie says in his book

Transylvania has always been separate from Hungary in its traditions, though the Magyars were in the ascendancy; it has always been a centre of toleration and religious liberty in comparison with other parts of the country. But this toleration extended only to the Magyars, Saxons and Szekels (Szeklers). The Wallachs were considered a subject race, for they were not of noble blood, according to their masters.

In a country where travellers were few (Charles Boner found as he travelled through Transylvania in 1863 that many of the people had never seen a foreigner and the solitary Englishman who lived in Sibiu when Mrs Gerard was there in the 1880s was the talking point of the town), the Saxon settlements must have seemed to the foreigner oases of civilization in what Boner called 'the odd corner in Europe' and 'the unknown land'. It is worthy of note that even today Snow can state that Romania is 'still mysterious' for English readers.

It must be galling to the modern Romanians, with their great achievements, to read about the standard of living to which they were reduced in Transylvania just over a century ago. Boner said that 'The Wallachian villages [he uses the term in the sense of Romanian] always reminded me of Robinson Crusoe's settlement, so coarsely were they built, and as if in their construction the various appliances of civilized life had been entirely wanting, which was in reality the case.' Elsewhere he describes the neat stone houses of the Saxons and compares them with the dilapidated cottages of the Romanians which adjoin them:

Now comes a succession of unwieldy dwellings. The walls bulge in different places; there is no sharpness in the forms; all indicates a low grade of civilisation. The windows are small; the gate, uncouthly painted, is put together with wooden nails; you probably do not perceive a single thing in which iron has been employed. The whole house is wattled, and when finished is whitewashed over.

It is exactly the architecture that a wrecked mariner, or a wanderer
in the forest with his axe, would resort to, were he to build himself
a dwelling.

Poor Romanians! These were the 'gifted people', in Snow's
phrase, reduced to abject straits. But the gipsies were in an even
worse plight. Boner continues:

> The gipsy settlements struck me as particularly wretched. Though
> cold and frosty, children of ten or twelve years of age stood outside
> the huts without a particle of clothing. In that state they will often
> sit on a piece of ice, and with feet drawn together, slide down a
> frozen slope. Many die, however, from exposure and privation;
> but the first years once over, their hardened frames bear every
> inclemency.

Not only did the gipsies survive; they flourished up to the
outbreak of the second world war. There is not the same evidence
of their settlements in Transylvania today.

When Boner was in Transylvania the Saxons were already
in decline. Their numbers were not increasing, the Romanians
were taking over the land they had tilled and even their trade.
Boner remarked that 'The trade with Wallachia and further
eastwards has passed entirely out of the hands of the Saxons
and into those of the Wallachian merchants of Kronstadt
(Braşov).' The ancient national status of the Saxons was abolished
in 1876. Still, old attitudes die hard. A few years ago I was in
a restaurant in Sibiu when a rather drunken row broke out
among a party of men accompanied by a solitary girl at a neighbouring table. My interpreter explained that she was engaged to
one of the men who was being asked by his companions how he,
a member of a noble race (presumably Saxon) could marry someone so inferior to him; she came from Craiova, in southern
Romania. I was surprised that she did not get up and walk out.

The historical Dracula's raids against Braşov and Sibiu in
Transylvania were, of course, accompanied by a certain amount
of risk because of the possibility of Hungarian intervention, but
the raids against the Turks were risky in the extreme because, to
a certain extent, he held his throne with their permission. The

Ottoman power began to expand at the time of Mircea the Old, who, although victorious at the Battle of Rovine in 1394, was forced by the numerical superiority of the Turks to withdraw with his troops over the Carpathians to Braşov, whence he returned in the spring, together with the army of King Sigismund of Hungary, which included a Transylvanian contingent of considerable size. Mircea the Old was described by a Turkish chronicler as 'the most valiant and shrewd of Christian princes', and some of his bravery and skill was inherited by his grandson, Dracula.

After two decades of continued anti-Turkish resistance, Mircea, recognizing the overwhelming numerical superiority of the Turks, was forced into paying a tribute to the sultan, but unlike Bulgaria, which was under Turkish domination for five hundred years, Wallachia was able to keep a native administration and an independent native church – the churches were not converted into mosques, as happened in the larger centres in Bulgaria – the nobility lost none of its lands, and no Turk was allowed to settle on Romanian soil.

The Hungarians were having their own difficulties with the Turks. After Mircea the Old, Iancu of Hunedoara, better known as John Hunyadi, the powerful governor of Transylvania, regent of Hungary (1446–56) and father of the great King Matthias Corvinus, was the second leader of European standing produced by the Romanian people; the third was Stephen the Great, Dracula's cousin. Hunyadi engaged in many battles with the Turks and was a prominent crusader, but was enraged when Vlad Dracul, Dracula's father, allowed the Turks to have access to Transylvania in 1442, and, after their defeat near Sibiu, chased them into Wallachia and Dracul off his throne.

The story of Turkish-Transylvanian-Wallachian relations is too long and complex to be told in detail here, but it is important to note that after the Battle of Mohács in 1526, when the Turks decisively defeated the Hungarians, Transylvania was completely severed from Hungary and set up as a separate principality, but even before this Transylvania had had its own judicial and administrative life. The political status of Transylvania after Mohács was similar to that of Wallachia and Moldavia, the other Romanian lands, as all three were under Turkish suzerainty.

The Habsburg dynasty of Austria now comes into the picture. The *voivode* of Transylvania, John Zápolya, who was elected King of Hungary in 1526, engaged Transylvania in a twelve-year war against Ferdinand, the Habsburg claimant to the Hungarian throne. Afterwards Hungary was divided between the Habsburgs and the Turkish sultan, and it was then that Transylvania was transformed into an autonomous principality. Turkish power began to wane in the following century. The Turks were defeated before Vienna in 1683, and the Transylvanians, their lands overrun by the emperor's troops, recognized under the Treaty of Vienna in 1686 the suzerainty of the Habsburg Emperor Leopold I. Transylvania was officially attached to Habsburg-controlled Hungary and the prince of the country was forced to accept the protection of the Austrian emperor.

In more modern times, 1848 was a turning point in Romanian history. Europe was then in ferment. France was proclaimed a republic again after the abdication of King Louis Philippe and revolution spread to Hungary, Bohemia and the Romanian lands. In Vienna there was a popular uprising and in Pest the anti-Habsburg revolt marked the beginning of the 1848-9 revolution. There were revolutions in Moldavia and Wallachia, but let us concentrate on Transylvania and the conflicting interests of the revolutionaries there. The Romanians wanted autonomy under the Empire but the Hungarians, disregarding the wishes of the Romanians, who were in the majority, voted at the Diet of Transylvania at Cluj for the union of the Transylvanian principality with Hungary.

Fighting between Romanians and Hungarians broke out in Transylvania in the autumn of 1848, but the main conflict was yet to come. Early in 1849 the Hungarian Army, led by General Joseph Bem, conquered all Transylvania except the region of the Apuseni Mountains which was guarded by a peasant army led by Avram Iancu. Until the Tsarist troops summoned to the aid of the Habsburgs passed into Hungary and Transylvania to stifle the revolution, the people's army of the Moți (the Romanians from

the Apuseni Mountains) inflicted several defeats on the Hungarians, who, recognizing that they could not fight both Russians
and Romanians, signed a peace draft which restored to the
Romanians some of their rights. Romanians and Hungarians
were now pledged to fight together, but by the autumn of 1849
the revolution was crushed, and Transylvania became a province
in the Habsburg Empire, led by a governor with his residence in
Sibiu and directly subordinate to the Court in Vienna. The revolution in Wallachia had been crushed by the Turks in the previous year.

The Austrians treated all nationalities in Transylvania with
equal severity, but in the other two Romanian lands the situation
was somewhat better. The Romanians achieved their first real
step towards national unity in 1859, when Wallachia and
Moldavia combined under Prince Alexandru Ioan Cuza, a par-
ticipant in the 1848 revolution. Thus union was recognized by
the great powers, but the political situation did not allow for full
independence, as the territories were under the Turks. In 1877,
however, the Romanians combined with the Russians in fighting
the Turks. Romanian armies crossed the Danube and won a
number of victories, thereby repaying old scores. With the defeat
of the Turks the yoke of centuries slipped from Romanian
shoulders, and in that year Romania as a truly independent
country was born, albeit a country of only two of the states,
Wallachia and Moldavia.

Difficulties continued in Transylvania. In 1849 the Emperor
Franz Joseph 1 had promulgated a constitution by which he
recognized Transylvania's limited independence. The Diet of
Transylvania was convened at Sibiu in July 1863 and now, for
the first time, the Romanians sent the greatest number of delegates, but only two years later the Diet was transferred to Cluj,
where it voted for the annexation of Transylvania to Hungary,
despite Romanian protests. In 1867 the Austrians and Hungarians
reached an agreement on the creation of the Austro-Hungarian
dual state under which Transylvania, until then under the direct
administration of the emperor in Vienna, was incorporated into
Hungary.

Up to the outbreak of the first world war a programme of
Magyarization was carried out in Transylvania, and the Saxons,
who had lost their centuries-old privileges as well as their national
status, suffered with the Romanians. Modern Romania, in the
sense that we know it today, was born after the end of the 1914–
18 war, when the ramshackle Austro-Hungarian Empire fell to
pieces. Romania had entered the war on 14–17 August 1916 on
the side of the Allies who, first by the convention of 18 Septem-
ber/1 October 1914 and later by the formal Treaty of 17 August
1916, had recognised Romania's rights to those territories within
the Austro-Hungarian monarchy inhabited by Romanians. In
1920 the Allies confirmed the union in the Treaty of Trianon.

In July 1940 Hungary took advantage of the international
situation to press its claims to Transylvania, which had never been
dropped, and forced Germany and Italy to impose the Vienna
award, which restored to Hungary about two-fifths of the en-
larged Transylvania, with a population of about 2,500,000,
composed of Magyars and Romanians in equal numbers. The
Allied-Romanian armistice of 12 September 1944 promised
Romania the restoration of 'all or the greater' part of the territory lost to it. The peace treaty of 10 February 1947 finally re-
established the 1920 Romanian-Hungarian border.

Transylvania, then, is a land which has been under the control of Turks, Hungarians and the Austro-Hungarian Empire
administered from Vienna. It was swept by the migration of barbaric tribes after the withdrawal of the Roman legions and by
the great Mongol invasion of 1241. The Hungarians were there
in strength for nearly one thousand years and the Saxons maintained their position of privilege for six hundred years. During
these centuries the Romanians, who always comprised the bulk
of the population, maintained their distinctive way of life which
only now is achieving full expression.

On 30 December 1947 Romania was proclaimed a People's
Republic and on 21 August 1965 a new constitution was adopted
that proclaimed The Socialist Republic of Romania so that it
is now a Communist country. This is not an ideology that has been
forced on the people. More than a century ago Boner, a shrewd

observer of the political scene, noted that 'the political creed of
the Romanians of Transylvania is communistic' (he uses a small
c). The Communism applied in Romania is, it must be admitted,
of an orthodox and rigid kind, but there is a reason for this.
Romania has a large boundary with the Soviet Union and does
not want to share the experience of Hungary and Czechoslovakia,
two countries which, as a result of Soviet intervention, now have
Russian troops stationed on their soil.

Romania, although a member of the Warsaw Pact, has taken
an independent line on many occasions, such as when she refused to invade Czechoslovakia in 1968, and has not always followed Russian foreign policy, as in the ideological dispute with
China. Efforts by the high command of the Warsaw Pact forces
to hold troop exercises on Romanian soil have always been refused. The realistic thinking of the Romanians is that no soften-
ing of the 'party line' should serve as an excuse for the Soviet
Union to mount an invasion and once again establish a garrison in Romania; there have been no Russians troops there since
1958.

There were disputes about the role Romania was to play in the
East European Communist Bloc in 1962 when efforts by
Romania to advance industrialization were opposed by the Soviet
Union which, as principal member of what is known in the West
as Comecon (the Council for Mutual Economic Assistance)
wanted to operate the principle of 'the socialist division of labour
on an international scale', the idea being that the countries of
Comecon were to be mutually supporting and dependent, and
that each country would do the thing it did best. Obviously, this
meant that most countries would have to scale down any plans for
diversification, and the realistic Romanians feared that their role
was to be a granary and a supplier of raw materials for the more
industrialized Communist countries, in particular Russia, and in
return to be a recipient of their finished products. As a result
mainly of Romanian opposition to the concept of Comecon
being used as an instrument of supranational policy, a meeting
of Comecon leaders in Moscow in June 1962 announced that
the work of co-ordinating national economic plans was to be

delayed, dropped the idea of supranationalism and reinstated the idea of bilateral agreements.

Romania could now awake from the sleep of centuries. Transylvania in particular had been backward for a country so rich in mineral resources and with a fertile soil. There were various reasons for this: poor communications; lack of co-ordination of resources (Boner reported a profusion of good wine but not nearly enough casks or bottles for it); the prolongation of a feudal system that had long outlived its purpose; failure to provide an outlet for the creative potentialities of the general population; and inefficiency. These deficiencies, and the disturbances that followed as a result, were not confined to Transylvania. As late as 1907 Romanian peasants rose in revolt and King Carol mobilized the army to suppress the uprising. Thousands of peasants – certainly more than 10,000 – were killed.

Romania now has one of the strongest economies in Europe, with a national growth rate of between 9 and 10 per cent and up to 14 per cent in some sectors. At the end of the 1971–5 Plan the overall industrial output had risen 84 per cent as against the 1970 level. Romania's industrial output per head now equals the peak industrial output of 30 pre-war Romanians. You do not find the profusion of consumer goods such as there are in the shops of Western capitals or regional towns, but a reason for this is that the returns from industry are ploughed back into it to cater for expansion. In Transylvania in the middle of the last century 87 per cent of the population was occupied with husbandry. 'As long as the dwellers in the land were in a state of vassalage, they had little interest in cultivating their fields, or in making them produce more than sufficed', Boner wrote in the 1860s. 'Serfdom is at an end; but the state of mind engendered by it still exists, and its evil influence with regard to husbandry will only gradually die out.' As a result of the country's accelerated drive for industrialization, the percentage of the total employed population engaged in agriculture in Romania has declined from 74.1 per cent in 1950 to just over 49 per cent in 1970. In 1975 almost 60 per cent of the total working population was engaged in activities other than agriculture, and by the end of the

next two decades it is expected that only about 20 per cent of
Romania's work force will be on the land.

Romania's economic progress has been remarkable, not least in
some centres connected with the historical Dracula. 'Poverty
reigns in Transylvania, but it is a distinguished poverty', Dr
Starkie wrote after his visit there in 1929. The old Transylvania
is changing, however. People come home from working on a
collective farm or in a factory not to listen to tales round the
fireside but to watch television. Yet away from the beaten track
old beliefs still linger, beliefs that were old when Dracula, the
scourge of the Turks, was young. It is ironical that people who
have never heard of Transylvania, with its long traditions and
its figures of international reputation, have heard of the fictional
Dracula; indeed, who has not? So to the public at large Transylvania means Dracula, and the fictional Dracula leads back into
the mists (and myths) of history and to the real Dracula.

2 Dracula in fiction

It can be argued that *Dracula*, which Bram Stoker first published in 1897 and had reprinted many times, introduces he who has become the best-known character in English fiction, more famous even than Conan Doyle's Sherlock Holmes. People who seldom open a book have seen Count Dracula on films. He was described by Bram Stoker as

a tall old man, clean shaven save for a long white moustache, and clad in black from head to foot, without a single speck of colour about him anywhere. . . . His face was a strong – a very strong – aquiline, with high bridge of the thin nose and peculiarly arched nostrils with lofty domed forehead, and hair growing scantily round the temples, but profusely elsewhere. His eyebrows were massive, almost meeting over the nose, and with bushy hair that seemed to curl in its own profusion. The mouth under the heavy moustache was fixed and rather cruel-looking, with peculiarly sharp white teeth; these protruded over the lips, whose remarkable ruddiness showed astonishing vitality in a man of his years.

The reference to the protruding teeth is significant. Count Dracula was a vampire. Let us consider some of the possible reasons for the continued (and growing) Dracula cult, which so mystifies the Romanians.

Charles Davidson, who reviewed Daniel Farson's *The Man who Wrote Dracula, a Biography of Bram Stoker* in *The Times Literary Supplement*, mentioned that over 400 films have been devoted to the Dracula theme and pointed out that

Not even Holmes, risen from the Reichenbach Falls, has spawned such a cult; not Scarlett O'Hara herself owes so much to the film industry. If all the people who have ever heard of Emma Bovary,

of Raskolnikov, of Felix Krull, of Colonel Newcome, were put
together, they probably would not amount to a tenth of those
familiar with the name of the Transylvanian Count, who so
abundantly justifies Pirandello's remarks about the reality of the
fictitious. He represents, as Stevenson's Mr Hyde represents, an
element in the human condition, partly sexual, partly derived from
that desire to transcend death so differently treated by Bram
Stoker's fellow Dubliner Swift, in his creation of the Struldbrugs,
and Shaw, in *Back to Methuselah*. Unlike the Struldbrugs, of
course, Dracula did not simply age without dying, but perpetually
renewed his youth by drinking blood from the living : a loathsome
elixir.

What better indication of a cult can there be than *The
Annotated Dracula* which has an exact reproduction of the text
from the first edition and numerous notes? The author,
Transylvanian-born Leonard Wolf, a professor of English at San
Francisco State University who has conducted courses on *Dracula*,
says that the book is one of the most terrifying in the world.

Professor Wolf considers that the book is also, as a literary experience, one of the strangest since it gives wildly contradictory
signals about what kind of book it is.

Certainly it is a horror tale in which there is plenty of that fearful, grisly, wonderful and sometimes silly stuff that we count on
finding in our blood-and-gore late bedtime reading. On the other
hand, from its pages there rise images so dreamlike and yet so
imperative that we experience them as ancient allegories. Everywhere one looks, there flicker the shadows of primordial struggles,
the perpetual tension between the dark and the light; the wrestling
match between Christ and Satan; and finally, the complex allegories
of sex : sex in all its unimaginable innocence, or sex reeking with
the full perfume of the swamp. And all these urgencies are seen or
sensed through a hot wash of blood which, deny it though we will,
fascinates us very nearly to the point of shame.

Professor Wolf's contention that the book concerns 'the perpetual tension between the dark and the light' was confirmed
by the decision of the United States Army to issue free paper-
back copies of Stoker's *Dracula* to the troops serving overseas.

B

Gabriel Ronay, another Transylvanian-born writer, pointing this out in *The Dracula Myth* says that

Count Dracula, it was argued by academics and politically-minded psychologists, represents the expansionist forces of Eastern Europe which seek to destroy, through violence and internal subversion, the democratic fabric of western civilisation. The count's interest in disorder and violence – the bogey of the law-abiding American citizen – was given special emphasis, and by way of proof it was pointed out that Jonathan Harker, Stoker's mouthpiece in the novel, had noted that the laws and customs of the West did not apply to Dracula's world.

Although the Americans had an ideological interest in using Dracula as a weapon in cold war politics, this represents only a tiny fraction of the worldwide preoccupation with Dracula, stimulated by commercial interests, it is true, but these can only reflect public tastes. Some of these commercial interests are aimed at the small boy or girl in the form of black ice lollies or in figures of Dracula in a ‘great monsters’ series, but the major section of the Dracula industry (there is no other word for it) consists of continual reprinting of the book, which is now out of copyright, translations (Dracula has been published in many languages), plays, films and documentaries on the Dracula theme, and now conducted tours to ‘Dracula country’ in Romania, and in particular Transylvania. These tours have attracted visitors from countries as distant from Transylvania as Japan, Australia and New Zealand.

Bram Stoker's interest in Transylvania was stimulated when he met Arminius Vambery, professor of Oriental languages at the University of Budapest, in London in 1890 and heard from him accounts of folk beliefs in eastern Europe, particularly those of Transylvania, the Latin name of which signifies 'The land beyond the forest', ie from Hungary. Vampire stories were popular then, one of the best being Le Fanu's *Carmilla*, published in Dublin in 1872 and Stoker, after a dream about a vampire king rising from his tomb, set about creating his own ghoul. Doubtless influenced by his talks with Vambery, Stoker chose Transyl-

vania for the setting of his story, stating through his mouthpiece
Harker that 'every known superstition in the world is gathered
into the horseshow of the Carpathians', and now he needed a
ghoul to fill the central role. In the course of his research at the
British Museum he came across gruesome and bloody tales of a
fifteenth-century Prince of Wallachia, Vlad Tepeş (Vlad the
Impaler) also known as Dracula, and *Dracula* was born.

Some of the tales about the historical Dracula are truly horrify-
ing, but Stoker was not to know that most of them had been dis-
seminated by Saxons, long resident in Transylvania, and were
greatly exaggerated. Stoker did not go to Transylvania and does
not seem to have done any deep historical research. He makes
Count Dracula declaim on the virtues of the Szeklers (Szekelys
in the book) and refer to them as 'We Szekelys', but the historical
Dracula was a Romanian, not a Szekler. The Szeklers, a population derived from Turkish and Oriental elements, who were
living alongside the Hungarians as far back as the times when the
latter were still pagan, were settled by the Hungarians on the
borders as guards against the invasions from the east. The Count
would, in a sense, be speaking in accordance with his rank when
he told Harker, 'Here I am noble; I am boyar; the common
people know me, and I am master', but the historical Dracula
was a prince, 'a great ruler' in his own words, and he would
never think of putting himself among the boyars, whom he
regarded as subjects, treating them with excessive severity.

As Stoker had never been to Transylvania he could allow his
imagination to guide his words in painting a dramatic landscape
in keeping with the theme of his novel. The Count's castle is
placed near the Borgo (Bîrgău) Pass in north-eastern Transylvania, a lonely spot even today, and although the ruins of a castle
have been found in this vicinity there is nothing to connect it
with the historical Dracula. Transylvania was then so remote, and
visited by so few travellers, that any novelist who wanted to startle
his readers with a Gothic horror story was drawn to the country,
and could write as he pleased about it without much fear of con-
tradiction.

Quite apart from *Dracula* addicts, there are followers of Jules

Verne's novel *The Castle of the Carpathians* who also want to visit Transylvania. Verne delighted in describing the beautiful scenery of the country, 'the old region of the Dacians', and as he favoured Romanian national aspirations ('These Wallachians in Transylvania have not despaired of shaking off the yoke, the future belongs to them', a sentiment shared by Mrs Gerard), the novel is understandably popular in Romania and has been widely read there. French tourists and others take part in a coach tour, 'Following in the steps of Jules Verne', in the course of which they visit spots such as Hunedoara Castle and Sibiu associated with the historical Dracula as well as the French writer. Although Dracula tours are sponsored by the Romanian Ministry of Tourism, and are increasingly popular, Stoker's novel has never been published in Romania nor are Dracula horror films screened there. Westerns are popular in Romania, but sex and horror films and those considered to encourage violence are banned. This view is perhaps understandable. The science fiction writer Brian Aldiss, reviewing *The Annotated Dracula* in *The Guardian,* said that 'Like Frankenstein at the beginning of the century, Dracula has been on the rampage ever since, appeasing that fundamental human desire to be scared to the limits of our wits. . . . Stoker's good plain style, his well-managed set pieces, and of course the whole macabre invention with its gamey sexual overtones, makes *Dracula* one of the best nasty reads in the language.'

Although the Dracula industry has, understandably, the enthusiastic support of the Romanian Ministry of Tourism, I have found officials there embarrassed by the emphasis placed by Western writers on Dracula as a vampire and by accounts of vampirism in Transylvania. This embarrassment is shared by leading scholars whom I interviewed. Most writers seem to have confused vampirism with the old Romanian folk belief that bodies may leave the grave after death as 'ghosts' but not to suck blood. Historians view the Western interest in Dracula with suspicion, suspecting that the vampire of Stoker's novel could be confused with a prince of Wallachia who, although not a leading figure such as Michael the Brave or Stephen the Great in the pantheon of Romanian heroes, has a respected place there for his feats against the Turks.

Readers may wonder how a *voivode* of Wallachia – the word generally means ruling prince but the title may also be used for governor and occasionally duke – called Vlad and known as the Impaler to distinguish him from others of the same name can also be called Dracula. Let Professor Constantin C. Giurescu, a leading Romanian historian, explain. 'I'd like to say from the very first that Dracula is not a nickname. Dracula is his name. He calls himself that in a letter. And in Romanian Dracula means "son of the devil" – his father being Vlad Dracul.' I will trace Dracula's family connections in the next chapter, and explain why his father was known as Vlad the Devil (or Dragon), but as Bram Stoker had quite clearly based his character of the vampire Count on an historical personage of some note the fears of the historians of a confusion of identity are justified.

Dracula had three reigns but two were so brief that they may be disregarded. Shortly before his principal reign began, the fall of Constantinople to the Turks sent shivers of apprehension through Christendom. Dracula carried out some brilliant campaigns against the Turks, but what reputation he gained by this was more than lost by the campaigns of villification by the pamphleteers. The reasons for this included his widespread use of impalement as a psychological weapon. Dracula did not invent this form of execution nor was it confined to him during his lifetime : it was the scale of his impalements that caused horror, and when used against Saxons, whether in trade disputes or for harbouring claimants to his throne, the news was quickly spread throughout Europe.

One extraordinary coincidence links the historical and fictional Draculas – both were the subjects of best sellers. The fictional Dracula, we have seen, is a cult figure and *Dracula* is a best seller, although the book made little money for the author in his lifetime. If the historical Dracula had lived a century earlier the accounts of his reigns, military exploits and impalements would have been confined to manuscripts in monkish Latin, but the invention of the printing press changed all that. Europe then as now had a population avid for horror stories and what better subject for these stories than the ruler of Wallachia, unpopular with the Hungarian Court, the Saxons of Tranyslvania and, naturally, the Turks? The first book in Romanian, the language of the people, was not to be published until 1554, so that the charges of cruelty went unchallenged in print.

According to Professors Florescu and McNally in their book *Dracula*,

In 1480 the first Dracula newssheet was circulating in the German world in the vernacular. Within two decades thirteen editions of the first version of the Dracula horror story were printed at Leipzig, Augsburg, Stuttgart, Strasbourg and Nürnberg, *perhaps the first best sellers in history* [my italics]. Whereas German pamphlets were possibly intended to blacken Dracula's reputation, or perhaps, simply to frighten or to amuse the reading public, in Russia the Dracula narrative was turned into an instrument justifying the despotism of Ivan III.

In France interest in Dracula, under his name Vlad, had developed from Dracula's own day when Walerand de Wavrin had fought in Vlad Dracul's army and had known Dracula as a young man. In general, Dracula was known in French literature as Vlad *l'Empaleur*, a ruler who was cruel, but only to his enemies. Victor Hugo presented him in one of his poems as a valiant fighter against the Turks.

Gabriel Ronay says that

Dracula became the talking point of central Europe. Leading printers of the time in search of financially rewarding secular stories seized upon it and more copies were printed than of the Bible, the best seller of the century [the fifteenth]. . . . Together with Columbus's letters about the discovery of the New World, and the French King's Italian campaigns, Dracula's heinous crimes became the favourite reading matter of Europe.

There was thus plenty of material about the historical Dracula in the British Museum Library, although much of it would be exaggerated and out of balance, for Bram Stoker's purposes when he set about creating a ghoul.

One of the strangest stories to come out of eastern Europe, or, indeed, of any part of the world, was available then for Stoker's purposes, and if he had come across it in the British Museum we might never have had *Dracula*. It concerns Countess Elisabeth Báthory, a famous society beauty, who believed in the magic properties of human blood, particularly that of virgins, for restoring her beauty, and to this end she tortured and killed 650 girls at Csejthe Castle in north-western Hungary and at her other residences. Such a story sounds unbelievable, but it is amply attested in court records which are still in existence.

As this is a book about Transylvania some mention of the 'Blood Countess', as she was called, is relevant, because the Báthorys were a great family in Transylvanian history, a number holding the post of governor. Stephen Báthory, for instance, was commander-in-chief of the forces which set out from Transylvania to restore Dracula to his throne in Wallachia. A later Stephen Báthory laid siege to Sighişoara, where Dracula was born. There was a strain of madness in this family which no doubt helps to explain Countess Elisabeth's exploits. In 1608 Gabriel Báthory was appointed governor of Transylvania – 'Transylvania's Pestilence', as the old chronicles name him, or 'The Madman' as he was called by the Turks. He was deposed by the Sultan before he carried out his threat to kill every man, woman and child in Sibiu, a town from which he extorted every florin he could. 'He was a very Nero, regardless of law and humanity, whose chief joy was to inspire fear and dread', said Charles Boner. Another governor (or prince) of Transylvania was Sigismund Báthory (1572–1613), who offered his throne to the Emperor Rudolph II so that he might take Holy Orders. He changed his mind and tried to regain his throne, but his army of Poles and Cossacks was routed by Michael, *voivode* of Moldavia (Michael the Brave) at Suceava in 1600. 'Báthory's indisputable genius must have been warped by a strain of madness', it is stated in the *Encyclopaedia Britannica*. 'His incalculableness, his savage cruelty (like most of the princes of his house he was a Catholic and persecutor) and his perpetual restlessness point plainly enough to a disordered mind.' This was indeed a strange family in which

Countess Elisabeth, who was born in 1560 in a part of Hungary bordering the Carpathian mountains, was not the only monster of cruelty.

Countess Elisabeth, engaged to be married at the age of eleven to Count Ferencz Nadasdy to suit the interests of two powerful Protestant families, was at the age of fourteen, while staying at the chateau of Countess Ursula Nadasdy, her future mother-in-law, suddenly spirited away by her own mother to one of the family's remotest castles in Transylvania. There she was kept in complete isolation on account of 'a contagious disease', and gave birth to a daughter rumoured to have been fathered by one of her peasant playmates. A local woman to whom the child was entrusted left the country for Wallachia with Elisabeth's bastard. The Báthorys made the woman and child a generous settlement, but they were forbidden to return to Hungary in the Countess's lifetime.

A few months later Elisabeth was married to Count Nadasdy. She bore him four children, but she also had lesbian tendencies, encouraged by her aunt, Countess Klara Báthory, a well-known lesbian, and began to torture servant girls, no doubt because of the sexual pleasure that resulted from these actions. In 1604, after her husband's death, her real atrocities began.

Elisabeth was afraid of becoming old and losing her beauty. One day a maid accidentally pulled her hair while combing it. Elisabeth slapped the girl so hard that she drew blood which spurted on to her hand. It immediately seemed to the Countess as if her skin in that area took on the freshness of that of her young maid. She then summoned her major-domo and man-servant who stripped the girl, cut her and drained her blood into a huge vat. This was the first of the Countess's blood baths, but many more were to follow.

Girls were enticed to the castle from considerable distances so that they could be killed for their blood. Some were even of noble birth. The Countess had a cylindrical iron cage – an 'Iron maiden' – built so that a naked girl could be forced inside it, and, recoiling from the stabs of a red-hot iron, impaled on the spikes. The blood ran down into a catchment area and, warmed over a slow fire, was used for the ritual bath at daybreak.

Rumours about the missing girls began to circulate. The Countess was questioned about the disappearances by the Lord Palatine, her cousin Count Thurzo, but although her accomplices quickly confessed to the murders, she denied them. The Count, on the orders of the King, returned to Csejthe Castle, and led by castle people who knew all the secret passages, was taken through the vast underground labyrinth to the Countess's torture chamber. There they found a big, fair-haired naked girl dead on the floor. Her hair was torn out by the handful, her breasts cut off, her thighs and genitals burnt and her skin torn to threads. The walls were splattered with blood and the clockwork machinery of the 'iron maiden' was still wound for long hours of work. Nearby the Count's party found two more naked girls, tortured and close to death. And there they discovered the Countess too. Lower down in a cave officials found several girls who had been held without food or water for the next torture session.

These details were related at the trial of the Countess's accomplices which opened at the small market town of Bicse, near Csejthe, on 2 January 1611. The Countess was spared the humiliation of a public trial because of her powerful family connections. After a five-day trial the mandatory death sentence was passed on her accomplices, but she was sentenced to be immured in the castle. Workmen walled in the windows and doors of a small room in which the Countess was confined, leaving only a food hatch to connect her to the outside world. She died on 14 August 1614, 'suddenly and without a crucifix and without light', in the words of a contemporary chronicler.

What a story to out-Dracula Dracula Bram Stoker could have made of this, particularly as Countess Elisabeth also dabbled in the occult!

3 The historical Dracula

Wallachia, which was to be ruled by Vlad the Third, or the Impaler (Dracula), on three separate occasions, but twice only briefly, was founded at the beginning of the fourteenth century by the merging of various political factions. This was carried out by the prince of the Argeş region, Basarab I. Transylvania also contributed to the founding of Wallachia. The surplus population, mainly Romanians but also the Saxons and Szeklers, crossed the Carpathians and settled the towns and villages on the southern side during the thirteenth century.

It was a very large country by east European standards if one added the two Transylvanian duchies of Făgăraş and Amlaş, over which the Prince of Wallachia ruled as feudal lord — altogether 48,000 square miles with a total population then of half a million inhabitants scattered in 3,200 villages and townships. Most lived in the hilly Carpathian districts, but Wallachia stretched to the Danube. The Danubian plain, in those days still covered by extensive forests, was sparsely populated because of the constant threat of invasion.

During the first half of the fifteenth century Wallachia was a theatre of conflict between Turks and Hungarians. Each of the two powers attempted to impose a prince faithful to its cause. The subjection of Wallachia to Hungarian rule and its use as a buffer state was strategically important to the Hungarians in Dracula's time because of the continuing advance of the Turks along the Danube. Belgrade was the last major fortified city on the Danube before reaching Buda, the Hungarian capital. Wallachia continued to maintain its autonomous national statehood and a semblance of national life, although the price of this was at times an official alliance with the Turks.

Changes of ruler were confusingly frequent. Mircea the Old, Dracula's grandfather and a great ruler from 1386 to 1418, had both legitimate and illegitimate sons, among the illegitimate being Dracula's father, Vlad Dracul, or Vlad the Devil or Dragon. He was not so named because of his devilish deeds (he has not gone down to posterity as a cruel man) but because he was a member of the Order of the Dragon in which he was invested in 1431 by the Roman Emperor Sigismund, King of Hungary and Bohemia. The insignia of this Order, a semi-monastic, semi-military organization devoted to fighting the Turkish infidels, consisted of a prostrate dragon, wings extended, hanging on a cross, with its tail curled round the head and its back cleft in two. Dracula simply inherited the name of his father, and was known as the son of the devil, or dragon.

After the death of Mircea's eldest son, Mihail I, the throne of Wallachia became the object of bitter dispute between his legitimate and illegitimate brothers, Radu II, 'the Bald', and Alexander I. An additional rival was Dan II, a cousin, whose successors, according to Professors Florescu and McNally in their biography of Dracula, 'maintained a lengthy feud with the descendants of Dracul which was so bitter in intensity that some historians were tempted to label it the Drăculeşti-Dăneşti feud, even though both protagonists were actually members of the same Basarab family.'

It is essential to bear this dispute in mind when we try to interpret the reason for some of Dracula's impalements. He was always ruthless in dealing with claimants to his throne or in his actions against towns which harboured or encouraged them.

Vlad II (Vlad Dracul) secured the throne of Wallachia in 1436 and took up residence in Tîrgovişte, the capital, bringing his wife and his three sons, Mircea (the elder), Dracula and Radu (the handsome) with him. Life was now very different from the provincial atmosphere of Sighişoara, a Saxon town in Transylvania, where Dracul had been living. The young Dracula began his apprenticeship for knighthood at Tîrgovişte, being taught swimming, fencing, jousting, archery, court etiquette and horsemanship, as were his brothers.

Vlad Dracul now began a balancing act between Turkish and Hungarian pressure on him. He sensed that the balance of power was moving to the Turkish Sultan Murad II, who had destroyed the independence of Serbia and Bulgaria, and he signed an alliance with him in 1437. In the following year the peasants of Transylvania rose in revolt and Dracul accompanied Murad II on one of his frequent incursions into Transylvania during which murder, looting and burning took place. This naturally angered the Hungarians, who wanted the Wallachian ruler to support the renewal of the crusades against the Turks, but he refused to commit himself.

Matters came to a head in 1442 when Dracul made the mistake of allowing Turkish troops to enter Transylvania through Wallachia. It is probable that he underestimated the military skill of John Hunyadi, Governor of Transylvania, who inflicted a crushing defeat on the Turks near Sibiu. The Turks were chased into Wallachia and when they returned to Turkey Dracul followed them with his family. He was not to stay long in exile, however. In the spring of 1443 he was re-established on the Wallachian throne with Turkish help. This time the Turks were not taking any risks with him. As the price for his throne he had to promise that he would not take part in any military action against his Turkish overlord, he was to pay the usual tribute, to which was also added the obligation of sending yearly contingents of Wallachian children who were to be trained for the Turkish janissary corps, the 'élite' of the Sultan's troops.

The Turks still had their doubts about Dracul's reliability, and to quieten these the Wallachian ruler made the difficult decision in the summer of 1444 to send his two younger sons, Dracula, aged twelve or thirteen (the exact year of his birth is not known), and Radu, aged nine, as a pledge for his future good conduct. The boys were held captive in a fortress in western Anatolia. Dracula was to remain there until 1448, a crucial period in his development. We must bear in mind, when assessing the reasons for Dracula's reputation for cruelty, the effects of his imprisonment by the Turks. In order to stay alive under extremely difficult circumstances (his father had sent a contingent of four

thousand Wallachian soldiers under his son Mircea to collaborate
with Hungarian and Polish armies in a new crusade which ended
in a disastrous defeat at Varna), Dracula had to learn guile and
to cope with the intrigues of the Turkish court. He also learnt the
Turkish use of terror as a psychological weapon, one he was later
to use against them, and Turkish military tactics, as well as the
language.

Dracul, in view of the Turkish victory at Varna, feared for the
lives of his sons. Even if their lives had been spared they could
have been blinded. The boys did not suffer any harm, although
attacks by the Christians continued, but it was not until 1446
that Dracul was told that his sons had been spared. The Turks
then offered to renew peace negotiations and a new treaty was
signed in the summer of 1447.

In the meantime, relations between John Hunyadi and Dracul
had deteriorated. Dracul and his son Mircea had blamed
Hunyadi for the débâcle at Varna; indeed Mircea had argued
for his trial and execution. In addition, Hunyadi had always
mistrusted Dracul's subservience to Turkish influence. The new
treaty with the Turks was probably regarded as fresh evidence
that Dracul was no longer a reliable ally of the Christian
crusaders. In view of this, Hunyadi led a punitive expedition
against Dracul in November 1447. A battle was fought some-
where south of Tîrgovişte, in which Dracul and Mircea were
overwhelmingly defeated. Dracul fled from the battlefield but
was pursued and killed in the marshes of Balteni, nor far from
Bucharest; his tomb has never been found. Mircea suffered an
even crueller fate. He was captured by enemy boyars – nobles or
large landowners – tortured and buried while still alive.

This event caused the Turks to reconsider the position of
Dracula and Radu. Wallachia was now firmly under Hungarian
control but Dracula, if helped to his father's throne, would surely
by an ally of the sultan. He summoned the two brothers to
Adrianople and told them that they were to be freed. Dracula
was given officer's rank in the Turkish army and waited in
readiness for a chance to invade Wallachia with Turkish support.
The expected opportunity occurred in the following year, 1448,

when Hunyadi was engaged in one of his expeditions against the
Turks with the support of the new ruler of Wallachia, Vladislav
II, and his army. In Vladislav's absence Dracula entered
Wallachia with Turkish support and took possession of the throne
at Tîrgovişte without a battle in the second half of October 1448.
He was in power for only a month, however, being defeated in
battle by Vladislav, who had Hungarian support.

Dracula returned to Turkey and the court of Murad II but
later went to Moldavia, where he was given a good reception at
the court of the ruler, Bogdan II, at his capital, Suceava. Here
he became friendly with his cousin, the future Stephen the
Great, who was to become Moldavia's most famous ruler.
Dracula's stay there was terminated in 1451 when the ruler was
assassinated. Stephen and Dracula fled to Transylvania and
threw themselves on the mercy of John Hunyadi. Dracula was
certainly not welcome. There is in existence a letter from Hunyadi
to the municipality of Braşov in which he advises the citizens of
that town, 'It is better that you capture him and chase him out
of the country'. Dracula returned to Moldavia in 1452 and
stayed there for three more years.

Circumstances were now changing in Dracula's favour. In
1453 Constantinople had fallen to the great Sultan Mohammed II
who was to feature so prominently in Dracula's later life.
Hunyadi was in dispute with Vladislav II over the duchies of
Făgăraş and Amlaş which he had removed from Wallachian
control, and no longer considered the Wallachian ruler a reliable
ally. When, in 1456, Dracula again sought refuge on Transylvanian soil because of internal developments in Wallachia
Hunyadi was able to consider his request more favourably than
he had before. Dracula was given the task of defending the
Transylvanian border against any enemy, Wallachian or Turkish,
and was introduced to the Hungarian king, Ladislas Posthumus,
as the only candidate who could be trusted as prince of
Wallachia. So Dracula, after being a protégé of the Turks, was
now to be an instrument of Hungarian policy in Wallachia.

Hunyadi died from the plague just outside Belgrade on 11
August 1456. He was a figure of European importance, judging

by the long entry devoted to him in the *Encyclopaedia Britannica* where he is described as 'one of Christendom's most glorious champions and also a great statesman'. When Jules Verne was in Transylvania in 1892 he found in the cottages highly-coloured portraits of Romanian patriots – 'amongst others the popular hero of the fifteenth century, the *voivode* Vayda-Hunyad', who was our John Hunyadi.

While a state of uncertainty existed in Transylvania after the governor's death Dracula seized his chance. He entered Wallachia at the head of a small contingent of his former subjects (there were no Hungarians in his army) and engaged Vladislav in battle on the Wallachian plain. Vladislav was put to flight and later killed at Tîrgşor (Tîrgşoru Vechi) on 20 August. On 6 September 1456 Dracula took the formal oath of allegiance to the Hungarian king and a few days later paid his formal act of vassalage in front of a Turkish delegation that had been sent to Tîrgovişte. Nothing could illustrate better Dracula's almost total reliance on the two great powers in the Balkans.

Features of Dracula's second reign were his stern action against the boyar class, his punitive expeditions against the Saxon merchants of Transylvania, and his battles with the Turks, all of them crammed into a reign which lasted only six years.

Although Transylvania was then part of the kingdom of Hungary, most of the inhabitants were Romanians, as was Dracula, and there was almost certainly an underlying resentment of the privileges extended to the Saxon traders in centres such as Sibiu and Braşov, both raided by Dracula. Little would have been heard of these raids outside the Balkans but for the scale of his impalements. Dracula, while a hostage of the Turks, had seen how a governor of Transylvania could take punitive action against his father, so why did he risk making raids into Transylvania, particularly when a monarch of the stature of Matthias Corvinus, Hunyadi's son, was on the Hungarian throne?

The answer, I feel, is that he knew the Hungarians resented the entrenched powers of the fortified Saxon cities. Charles Boner pointed out in his book on Transylvania that

These colonists were summoned to till the land, to defend it, and uphold the Crown. They came as freemen and as sole possessors of the soil on which they were to dwell; and they had the precaution to ensure their position by a treaty signed and sealed by the king, which succeeding rulers ratified anew. . . . There is at this moment in Europe (1863) no people, except the Swiss and the Belgians, enjoying such liberties and guaranteed rights as these Germans possessed when they settled in Transylvania.

But there was more to it than that. Relations between the two races were bitter and reminded Boner of the feeling existing between the English and French in Canada. 'There the two races do not blend, nor here either.' He added that 'the dislike – the hatred I may say – is felt most strongly for the Saxon of Hermannstadt (Sibiu); he is in truth different from those of other Saxon towns.'

Is it not possible that the Hungarian rulers, unable to take action against the stubborn Saxons with their insistence on their rights, looked the other way when Dracula went raiding? If it was the Hungarians who were raided in Transylvania there would have been an immediate reaction, I suggest. This is not a theory I have seen propounded before but I feel it is worth consideration.

Early in his reign Dracula signed a commercial treaty with Saxons in various areas of Transylvania, including Braşov and Sibiu, the two most important centres. The treaty contained provisions that Dracula would help to defend the Transylvanian Saxons against the Turks, but in the case of need, however, a stipulation gave him the right of asylum in Transylvania; the merchants were given the right to sell their goods and buy their raw materials unimpeded throughout Wallachia without localizing such transactions in specific towns as had been the practice; both sides undertook not to give protection to their political enemies and not to confiscate the goods of their respective merchants, no matter what the provocation.

Here again we have an example of the power of the Saxon-controlled trading towns. These municipalities assumed the right to give asylum to Dracula, a right, one would think, which would be exercised only by the King of Hungary or the governor of Transylvania acting on his behalf.

Dracula was soon involved in Transylvanian politics. He demanded the restoration of the duchies of Făgăraş and Amlaş which Ladislas Posthumus, the Hungarian king, considered an infraction of the treaty of submission signed in 1456. It is not surprising, therefore, that the king, sensing further insubordination, began once again to champion various anti-Dracula candidates. In addition, there were immediate members of his own family hostile to Dracula who were given support by the citizens of Sibiu.

The reign of Ladislas Posthumus was not to last long. A struggle for power broke out involving Matthias Corvinus, Hunyadi's son, who was to become one of the greatest figures in Hungarian and European history. The Saxons of Transylvania gave their support to Ladislas Posthumus and the Holy Roman Emperor Frederick III of Germany (Boner noted that the Germans retained links with their homeland and in times of struggle for the throne always sided with the German or Austrian claimant), but the final victory went to Matthias Corvinus, who succeeded to the Hungarian throne on 24 June 1458. The memory of this king lingered long in Transylvania. In his novel of Transylvanian life in the last century Jules Verne makes some of the action take place in an inn called the 'King Mathias'. Dracula had supported King Matthias, who showed his gratitude by writing to the citizens of Sibiu and asking them to change their political attitude to the Wallachian ruler, who was described as 'our faithful and beloved friend'.

King Matthias had cause to change his view of his 'faithful and beloved friend' in the next two years. Dracula, angered by the presence in Sibiu of hostile members of his family and claimants to his throne, carried out a lightning raid into that district in 1457, burning and pillaging castles and villages, with men, women and children perishing in the flames. A purpose of the raid may well have been that of capturing Vlad the Monk, Dracula's half-brother. Matthias Corvinus was not on the throne at the time, and he had his own cause for displeasure with the citizens of Sibiu, who were opposed to him, so that he probably cared little about what happened to the Saxons. He must have thought deeply, however, about the character and motives of the neighbouring ruler of Wallachia in the light of later events.

The good commercial relations with the Saxons were broken during the winter of 1458-9 when Dracula decided to increase the tariffs on Transylvanian goods in order to help local manufacturers. This was in violation of the treaty he had signed, and, worse still from the Saxons' viewpoint, he made them revert to the previous custom of trading only in certain specified towns such as Cîmpulung, Tîrgoviște and Tîrgșor. This closed many profitable centres and trading routes to the Saxons, who, accustomed to asserting their rights in Transylvania, decided to ignore Dracula's edict. For this they were made to pay dearly.

When in spite of Dracula's warnings (his letters are still in the archives at Brașov) the Saxons continued to send trading parties to areas in Wallachia where their rights had been withdrawn, quick retribution followed. A party of 400 young apprentices and some older merchants were apprehended at the old port of Brăila on the Danube and executed: one account says that they were assembled in a room and burned alive and another that they were impaled. Saxon sources say that the apprentices were 'mere boys who had come to Wallachia to learn the language', but to the Wallachians they were what we would call 'trade spies'.

More letters to the municipality of Brașov followed with warnings against harbouring claimants to Dracula's throne, particularly Dan III, known as Danciul. Dracula was to catch up with this particular pretender in the spring of 1460, and meticulous as ever in observing the niceties of such an occasion, forced him to read his own funeral oration and then decapitated him: his rank saved him from impalement.

Dracula raided Brașov in 1458 and 1459. On one raid he looted the thirteenth-century Saxon church of St Bartholomew on the outskirts of the town, the oldest in Brașov. This church still stands today. The atmosphere was peaceful when I stood in the graveyard among the flowers one summer, but it was easy to visualize how the invading forces could command it from the hill just above. Braşov is another town where you rub shoulders with the past. Vestiges found in the precinct of the town prove that it was already inhabited in the Neolithic era and that in the Iron age crowded Dacian settlements existed there. The written history of Braşov goes back to 1251. For centuries the carts of the Braşov merchants used to pass through the Carpathians into Wallachia, bringing cloth, metal and wax objects and taking back with them grain and cattle.

When the Turkish expansion became more evident in the fifteenth century the inhabitants of Braşov started to erect walls round their town. These walls were already there when Dracula made his first raid. On his approach the defenders retreated within the walls, but Dracula took prisoners, probably from those defending churches and other fortified buildings, and then burned the suburb of the town near the chapel of St Jacob.

One of the most publicized atrocities was the impalement of the prisoners of the raid on St Jacob's hill, 1,200 feet high, overlooking the town. The number of victims is not known, but they must have presented a grim sight to the inhabitants. It seems that it was on this site that Dracula was shown in two famous German prints wining and dining among the impaled corpses and apparently eating human remains, which could have suggested to Bram Stoker the theme of Dracula the vampire. As Professors McNally and Florescu point out in their biography of Dracula, 'Both the episodes and the associated woodcuts did more to damage Dracula's reputation than any other single pamphlet or print.' Stories about Dracula extended even to Russia. One Russian narrative tells how a boyar at Braşov with Dracula, apparently unable to endure the smell of coagulating blood any longer, had the misfortune to hold up his nose and express a gesture of revulsion. Dracula immediately ordered an unusually long stake for the would-be victim and presented it to him with the cynical remark: 'You live up there yonder, where the stench cannot reach you.'

When you pause in the weaver's bastion, which dates from the fifteenth century and is the best preserved of the seven bastions of the citadel, you can cast your mind back to Dracula's raids and the harvest of tortured bodies on the steep hill beyond. You can even study in the museum in the bastion a plan of the fortifications. As Dracula stood on the hill above Braşov he must have seen the famous black church in the process of construction : it was not finished until 1477, although building started almost a century earlier. This church, formerly Roman Catholic but now Lutheran, acquired its name after a great fire in 1689 which left nothing standing but the blackened walls, and is the largest in Romania, a monument to the days of faith. It is noted for a fine collection of Oriental carpets of the sixteenth and seventeenth centuries and for a large organ.

During the raids Dracula took care not to breach the walls. He wanted Braşov to remain a supplier of weapons and other goods. In modern times the town, which has a population of nearly 200,000, has become an important industrial centre, particularly for making tractors and lorries.

Other raids followed, Amlaş and Făgăraş, about which Dracula had been in dispute with the Hungarian king, being among those where there were many impalements, according to German accounts, but it is often difficult to assess the truth of stories told by monks and Saxon refugees. There is a continuing oral tradition that among the peasants and ordinary people Dracula had the reputation of being a just but severe ruler.

Dracula was always very conscious of his dignity. A celebrated painting by Theodor Aman captures the feeling of the occasion when Dracula ordered the turbans of Turkish envoys to be nailed to their heads. There are German, Russian and Romanian narratives of this. The Russian narrative is as follows :

At one time some envoys from the Turkish Sultan came to him; when they came and bowed to him according to their custom they did not take their turbans off. Dracula asked them : ' Why do you do this towards a great ruler?' They answered ' This is our custom, my Lord, which is that of our country.' Dracula then answered, 'I too wish to strengthen your law so that you may be firm ', and he ordered that their turbans be nailed to their heads with small iron nails. Then he allowed them to go, telling them : ' Go and tell your master that he is accustomed to endure such shame from you but we are not accustomed. Let him not impose his customs to other rulers, who do not wish them, but let him keep them in his land.

The Russian narrative further explains that

Whenever there came to him an envoy; from the Emperor, or from the King, if he was not properly attired and was not able to give answers concerning [Dracula's] punishments, he was impaled, being told : ' I am not guilty of your death, but your master, or you yourself; don't reproach me with anything, since your master, knowing you to be simple and uncultivated, has sent you to me, a wise ruler. Therefore, your master has killed you. But if you yourself have dared come to me on this mission, then you have killed yourself.'

Although the ruler of Wallachia owed allegiance to both Hungary and Turkey (he fell when the balance was broken) he was sovereign in his own country. But it is understandable that such high-handed behaviour as we have seen illustrated here would cause resentment and one day would reap a reckoning.

A number of Romanian folk tales stress not Dracula's cruelty but his sense of morality. One, translated by Professor Florescu from the Romanian, says that

When Dracula ruled Wallachia an important Florentine merchant travelled throughout the land, and he had a great deal of merchandise and money. As he reached Tîrgovişte, the capital of the country at the time, the merchant immediately went to the princely palace and asked Dracula for servants who might watch over him, his merchandise and his money.

Dracula ordered him to leave the merchandise and the money in the public square and to come to sleep in the palace. The merchant, having no alternative, submitted to the princely command. However, during the night someone passing by his carriage stole 160 golden ducats. On the next day, early in the morning, the merchant went to his carriage, found his merchandise intact, but 160 golden ducats were missing. He immediately went to Dracula and told him about the missing money. Dracula told him not to worry and promised that both the thief and the gold would be found. He ordered his servants to replace the gold ducats from his own treasury, but to add an extra ducat.

To the citizens of Tîrgovişte he ordered that they immediately seek out the thief and that if the thief were not found he would destroy his capital. In the meantime, the merchant went back to his carriage, counted the money once, counted it a second time and yet a third time, and was amazed to find all his money there with an extra ducat.

He then returned to Dracula and told him : ' I have found all my money, only with an extra ducat '. The thief was brought to the palace at that very moment. Dracula told the merchant : ' Go in peace. Had you not admitted to the extra ducat, I would have ordered you to be impaled together with this thief.' This is the way that Dracula conducted himself with his subjects, both believers and heretics.

In the Russian version of this story the merchant is a Hungarian. Another Russian story about Dracula, this time translated by Professor McNally, is that Dracula so hated evil in his land that if someone stole, lied or committed some injustice, he was not likely to stay alive. Whether he was a nobleman, a priest, a monk or a common man, and even if he had great wealth, he could not escape death if he were dishonest. He was so feared that the peasants say that in a certain place, near the source of the river, there was a fountain; at this fountain there came many travellers from many lands and all these people came to drink at the fountain because the water was cool and sweet. Dracula had purposely put this fountain in a deserted place, and had set a cup wonderfully wrought in gold and whoever wished to drink the water had to drink it from this gold cup and had to put it back in its place. So long as this cup was there no one dared to steal it.

There is a grotesque element in some of the stories about Dracula which have come down to us from Russian, German and Romanian sources. One, common to all three countries, is about the lazy woman. The Romanian version is that

Dracula was a man with grey matter in his brains and he insisted on good order in his state. Woe to any soldier whom he saw improperly attired, he rarely escaped with his life. He liked to see his citizens cleanly attired and looking smart. Around him, he could not tolerate anyone who floundered or was slow in his work. Whenever he noticed a libertine or a rake he lost his temper.

One day he met a peasant who was wearing too short a shirt. One could also notice his homespun peasant trousers which were glued to his legs and one could make out the side of his thighs when one saw him [dressed] in this manner. Dracula immediately ordered him to be brought to court. 'Are you married?' he inquired. 'Yes I am, your Highness.' 'Your wife is assuredly of the kind who remains idle. How is it possible that your shirt does not cover the calf of your leg? She is not worthy of living in my realm. May she perish!' 'Beg forgiveness, my Lord, but I am satisfied with her. She never leaves home and she is honest.' 'You will be more satisfied with another since you are a decent and hard-working man.'

Two of Dracula's men had in the meantime brought the wretched woman to him and she was immediately impaled. Then, bringing another woman, he gave her away to be married to the peasant widower. Dracula, however, was careful to show the new wife what had happened to her predecessor and explained to her the reason why she had incurred the princely wrath.

Consequently, the new wife worked so hard she had no time to eat. She placed the bread on one shoulder, the salt on another and worked in this fashion. She tried hard to give greater satisfaction to her new husband than the first wife and not to incur the wrath of Dracula. Did she succeed?

It is just as well that Dracula does not rule our country today, for he would have had to expend many stakes, which might have eliminated from our land the innumerable drones who wither the very grass on which they sit.

Dracula, we must remember, was a soldier and a brilliant one at that. His obsession with details of dress, whether that of envoys or peasants, is common to a certain type of military mind, although incomprehensible to others. From these folk tales about Dracula a recognizable personality emerges. Another aspect of his personality was his intense resentment of authorities who harboured claimants to his throne or who had harmed his family. He also resented any class which tried to share the privileges which, in his view, belonged only to the prince of the realm, or expected to exercise political power. Such a class was that of the boyars who had killed his brother Mircea and had supported the previous ruler Vladislav II. The cynicism of the nobles and landowning class towards their rulers was understandable. Such were the vacillations of politics in the Balkans, where the balance of power shifted between Hungarians and Turks, that the boyars concentrated on maintaining their own interests and privileges, all too conscious of the fact that in another year or two there would be another ruler on the throne or possibly a previous ruler restored.

Dracula waited three years before challenging the power of the boyars. He did it in a most deceptive manner by inviting them to a feast at his court at Tîrgovişte with their wives and families. When the festivities were well advanced the boyars were seized by palace guards and impaled outside the palace and beyond the city walls. Tradition has it that 500 boyars were exterminated in this way and an undisclosed number of women, but as Professors McNally and Florescu point out, 'the small size of the banquet hall at Tîrgovişte poses serious problems concerning the manner in which the boyars were seized (there was hardly room for 500 boyars in addition to Dracula's palace guard). One might imagine that on their way out of the palace the boyars were apprehended in the courtyard.' The young and able-bodied were marched off to Poenari and put to work on the rebuilding of Dracula's castle there. The extermination of the old boyar class meant that Dracula could create a new class of boyars who would be expected to be loyal to him. This was important in view of the conflict that was brewing with the Turks, particularly as bravery and ability in command in the field could now be rewarded in an appropriate way. In this we see once again a soldier's mind at work.

Relations with the Turks had been deteriorating while Dracula was concerned with consolidating his power, taming the boyars and dealing with the Saxons of Transylvania. Since the fall of Constantinople in 1453 pressure had been building up for a Christian crusade, but nothing had come of it. Possibly because he felt more in control of events inside his country, Dracula had been neglecting his treaty obligations with the Turks, which included the payment of 10,000 ducats every year, preferably brought by the prince in person, and a yearly visit to Constantinople to 'kiss the hem of the Sultan's coat tail' as a token of submission. It is not known whether Dracula did this after the first year or two of his reign, but if he did it would be in a cynical and realistic spirit: above all, Dracula was a realist.

Sultan Mohammed II was also a realist. He would be perfectly well aware of the pressures from the Pope for a crusade and, conscious of the type of prince who was now on the throne at Wallachia, would want to neutralize his influence. Hence, a summons to Dracula to go to Constantinople to explain why he had not paid the yearly tribute for the past three years nor had appeared in person. The Turks also made a new demand, a child tribute of five hundred young boys destined for the janissary corps, the infantry élite composed of recruits from other provinces of the Balkans. Dracula resisted this, and if Turkish recruiting officers appeared on Wallachian soil they were promptly chased away and, if caught, impaled as a deterrent to others.

Dracula refused to go to Constantinople on the grounds that if he did his enemies in Transylvania would seize power in his absence. In the meantime the Sultan was considering placing Radu the Handsome, Dracula's brother who was living in Constantinople and was of a much more amenable disposition than the ruler who had ordered the turbans of the Turkish envoys to be nailed to their heads, on the Wallachian throne, but he decided to give Dracula one more chance. He was invited to Nicopolis in Bulgaria to meet the governor, Hamza Pasha, who had been instructed to persuade Dracula to proceed to Constantinople, despite his previous reluctance to do so.

Dracula, sensing a trap that would result in his being taken captive, decided to meet cunning with cunning – how well he understood the eastern mind! After agreeing to proceed to the assigned meeting place, the Danubian port of Giurgiu (today an industrial centre with a population of 45,000), Dracula sent a consignment of cavalry there to hide under cover of the forests. In this ambush Dracula captured Hamza Pasha, the Sultan's chief envoy at the planned meeting, and another principal envoy, Thomas Catavolinos, a Greek, close to the fortress of Giurgiu which was built by Mircea the Old as a defence wall against the attacks of the Turks, but occupied by them in 1417. As the Turks opened the gates of the fortress on the orders of Dracula's men with the thought that only their own men would enter, the Wallachians, mixing with the Turks, also entered the fortress and, conquering it, set the town on fire.

We are fortunate to have Dracula's own account of this episode, sent to King Matthias Corvinus under the date of 11 February 1462. Dracula had been trying to arrange a marriage to one of the king's relatives, no doubt hoping that such an alliance with the Hungarian royal house would help to secure his hold on his throne. This account, accidentally found in the Munich archives in the 1920s by the Romanian historian, N. Iorga, states that

In other letters I have written to Your Highness the way in which the Turks, the cruel enemies of the Cross of Christ, have sent their envoys to me, in order to break our mutual peace and alliance and to spoil our marriage, so that I may be allied only to them and that I travel to the Turkish sovereign, that is to say to his court, and, should I refuse to abandon the peace, and the treaties, and the marriage with Your Highness, the Turks will not keep the peace with me. They also sent a leading counsellor of the Sultan, Hamza Bey of Nicopolis, to determine the Danubian frontier, with the intent that Hamza Bey should, if he could, take me in some manner by trickery or good faith, or in some other manner, to the Porte and if not, to try and take me in captivity. But by the grace of God as I was journeying towards their frontier, I found out about their trickery and slyness and I was the one who captured Hamza Bey in the Turkish district and land, close to a fortress called Giurgiu. As the Turks opened the gates of the fortress, on the orders of our men, with the thought that only their men would enter, our soldiers mixing with theirs entered the fortress and conquered the city which I then set on fire.

Hamza Bey and Catavolinos were beheaded at Giurgiu. The Turkish captives were escorted in chains to Tîrgovişte, stripped of their clothes in a meadow on the city's outskirts and impaled, joining the rotting bodies of the impaled boyars. This was how Dracula dealt with those who had incurred his wrath.

What could Dracula do next? He could no longer make peace

with the Sultan, or even negotiate with him, and he did not have
enough forces under his command, even allowing for the Bulgarian peasants who had joined his army, to wage war without
the support of allies, the principal of whom was Matthias
Corvinus. In order to impress the Hungarian monarch Dracula
sent him full details of his campaign along the Danube that
winter and, to stress the accuracy of his account, dispatched his
envoy, Radu Farma, with two bags of heads, noses and ears to
Buda.

During the winter of 1462 Dracula campaigned with his army
along the Danube up to the Black Sea, killing ' 23,884 Turks and
Bulgars without counting those whom we burned in homes or
whose heads were not cut by our soldiers' : the heads, apparently,
were regarded as trophies. Europe watched with admiration : it
seemed as if the days of the great Hunyadi had returned, and
once more a Christian crusader was harrying the infidel, freeing
the Balkans from the Turkish yoke and thereby guaranteeing the
freedom of the West, where the growing power of Islam had
been watched with apprehension since the fall of Constantinople.
The only practical support was given by Pope Pius II who sent
money, via Matthias Corvinus, to help the crusade, but this
never reached Dracula; it remained in the Hungarian royal
pocket.

Possibly Matthias Corvinus was doubtful about helping a
ruler who assessed enemy losses in terms of heads, noses and ears.
But Dracula did not give up hope of support from Hungary. He
wrote to Matthias Corvinus urging him to

Gather your whole army, your cavalry and your infantry, bring
them to our Wallachian land and accept to fight with us here. If
Your Highness does not wish to come personally, then kindly send
your army to the Transylvanian region of your realm . . . if Your
Majesty does not wish to give your army, then only send as many
as you wish, the Transylvanians and the Szekelys. And if Your
Highness is willing to lend help, then be good enough not to delay
our emissary [Radu Farma] who is bringing this letter to you. Send
him back to me immediately and swiftly. Let us in no way leave
unfinished what we have begun, let us push this affair to a con-

clusion. For if the Almighty will listen to the prayers and wishes of Christianity, if he will favourably listen to the prayers of his unworthy subjects, he will give us victory over the Infidel, the enemies of the Cross of Christ.

Despite this eloquent plea, Matthias Corvinus was not yet ready to move against the Turks, and Dracula found himself alone. He did what he could to hamper the Turkish invasion which he knew to be inevitable by destroying Danubian beachheads and port facilities as well as potential food supplies. Mohammed II left Constantinople on 26 April 1462 with the bulk of his army which has been estimated at 60,000 men, at least twice the size of the forces available to Dracula, who had not only been refused military aid by his cousin Stephen the Great, ruler of Moldavia, but who at this critical time had to divert forces to aid the fortress of Chilia on the Danube which was attacked by Stephen. The Turkish army included Prince Radu, whom the Sultan wished to place on the throne in Dracula's place, and 4,000 Wallachian horsemen.

The Turkish forces crossed the Danube on the night of 4 June in seventy boats and barges, despite fierce opposition from Dracula's forces, but after 120 guns had been transported this opposition lessened but not before 300 janissaries, who were in the spearhead of the attack, had been killed.

Dracula, aware that he could not defeat the Turks in open battle, withdrew towards his capital, leaving behind him empty villages and burnt fields. All too often the advancing Turks, seeking shade and shelter in a village, found only smoking ashes, and at night they had to defend themselves against guerilla raids by Dracula's horsemen, who swooped out of the forest and then melted back into it. Despite Dracula's harassment and scorched earth policy, the Turkish advance continued, but at Tîrgovişte the Sultan found the city abandoned, although the defenders were still manning the cannons. It should have been possible for the Turkish commanders to mount an attack that would have put the capital in their hands, but the Sultan, in his advance, had just come across a sight that profoundly shocked him. In a narrow gorge one mile long just outside the city there were the stinking remains of the Turks captured at Giurgiu and the boyars with their families impaled by Dracula. The number of those impaled is not known : a figure of 20,000 has been given, but this is probably too high. The Sultan knew only too well the use of terrorism as a weapon, but here was a practitioner of the art even more ruthless than he was. The Greek chronicler Chalkokondyles said that ' Even the emperor [Sultan], overcome with amazement, admitted that he could not win the land from a man who does such great things, and above all, knows how to exploit his rule and that of his subjects in this way.' He also related that the man who performs such deeds should be worthier of greater things. The 'greater thing' happened rather sooner than the Sultan expected.

Mohammed II now wanted time to reflect on his next move. He had advanced with his army in the burning heat of summer to find an empty capital, a forest of rotting corpses and an enemy who would never stage a 'set-piece' battle in which superior forces could be expected to prevail, and here we remember that the Sultan's forces were twice those of Dracula. In addition, plague had also appeared within the Turkish ranks. Before deciding on the next step, therefore, the Sultan camped for the night near Tîrgovişte, protected by ditches. It was then that Dracula mounted his famous night attack, a feat so daring that had it been successful, and it nearly was, his fame would have blazed throughout the Christendom of that time and down the ages.

While the Turkish camp settled down for the night Dracula held a council of war in a nearby village. He explained the plight of his capital, which could not be defended, and the risks of starvation : a scorched earth policy worked as much against his army as it did that of the Turks. His solution was to stage a night attack (a novel method of warfare at that time) on the Turkish camp and kill the Sultan. Several versions of what followed have been given by chroniclers, but apparently what happened is that, making use of Turkish prisoners who had been foolish enough to stray beyond the camp, Dracula made his way through the fortifications and then, with torches blazing, led the cavalry in a charge through the Turkish lines, slaying all in their path. There was utter confusion in the Turkish ranks and, if the other Romanian commander, a boyar named Galeş, had attacked from the other side of the camp as planned, victory would have gone to the Romanians. As it was, they nearly reached the gold-embroidered tent of the Sultan, but here the janissaries rallied and held the attack.

The Romanian effort had been dissipated by the cavalry making, in error, for the tent of the vizirs, Mohammed and Isaac, which they thought was that of the Sultan. Nicolas Modrussa, the papal legate to Pope Pius II, received in 1464 an account of the engagement from a veteran of Dracula's forces which could possibly have been dictated by Dracula himself. It said that

Dracula provoked an incredible massacre without losing many men in such a major encounter, though there were many wounded; he abandoned the enemy camp before daybreak and returned to the same mountain whence he had come, without anyone daring to follow him, since he had caused so much terror and trouble among all. I learnt by questioning those who had participated in this battle that the Sultan lost all confidence regarding the situation. During that night he secretly abandoned the camp and fled in a shameful way. And he would have continued in this way had he not been reprimanded by friends and brought back, almost against his will.

We will never know for certain whether the Sultan left his camp on the night of the attack or remained there, but he now decided to retreat with the bulk of his forces to the port of Brăila. He was a good enough soldier to realize that to move across the scorched Danubian plain in pursuit of an elusive enemy was to lengthen his supply lines and make them vulnerable to surprise attacks. Dracula, he probably reasoned, had made his last desperate throw and was unlikely to risk his forces on another night attack which by now had lost the element of surprise. He compromised by sending a portion of his forces, which included Prince Radu, in pursuit of Dracula. In this period of history there was nothing unusual in the concept of brother fighting brother. It was Mohammed II, a poet and a patron of the arts and of scholarship, who in his code of laws recommended his successors to kill their brothers on coming to the throne with a view to safeguarding the state in perpetuity from dynastic disputes. There is little doubt that Radu would have had Dracula executed if he had fallen into his hands.

We may pause here and say that Dracula's near success in the night attack, and the subsequent decision of the Sultan to retreat to Brăila, marked the Wallachian ruler's finest hour and the one by which he will be best remembered. After that it was downhill all the way, although, after a long interval, he was to occupy his throne briefly once more.

Nothing succeeds like success. If Dracula had been successful in his night attack the boyars who had taken to the hills with their families and their goods would have been the first to hail him, but their view of a dreaded ruler in retreat was very different; they threw off all pretence of support and looked for a new benefactor to restore to their class the rights and privileges which Dracula had removed.

When Sultan Mohammed in Brăila appointed Prince Radu as commander-in-chief with the mission of destroying Dracula and taking over his princely office, therefore, he gained the support of the boyars and through them their followers or dependents. Dracula proceeded with the main body of his army towards north-eastern Wallachia, but on his way several skirmishes took place with the Turks, Radu's forces and Moldavians, while Stephen the Great's forces were besieging the fortress of Chilia. These resulted in defeats for Dracula, but he gained two more victories, one in July and another in September. Time was running out for him, however, and the main towns were now under the control of Prince Radu and his Turkish masters. Dracula's army began to melt away and he had to think, not for the first time, in terms of asylum. In Turkey he would have been killed and to turn to his cousin Stephen would expose him, at that time, to being handed over to the Turks. This left only Transylvania. Dracula made his way there, not without great difficulty and in circumstances which are still obscure.

Dracula probably reached Transylvania in November, the

month in which Radu the Handsome, still residing at Brăila, was recognized as Prince of Wallachia by the boyar council and by King Matthias of Hungary, who had established his military headquarters at Braşov on 3 November 1462. Dracula, who might have expected to be received as a Christian hero – had not the courts of Europe thrilled to the tales of his exploits against the Turks during the previous winter? – was given a cool reception. There was for a time talk about a renewed crusade against the Turks (Matthias Corvinus was in possession of the Pope's money for this purpose) but negotiations broke down. On 26 November Dracula was apprehended by the Bohemian soldier of fortune, Jan Giskra, who was in the service of King Matthias, at the castle of Königstein (Piatra Craiului in Romanian) and brought back to Braşov. By 6 December King Matthias was on his way to Buda with his prisoner and Dracula retreats into obscurity for twelve years.

What was the reason for this drastic action against Dracula by King Matthias? Many theories have been advanced. One is that Dracula wrote to the Turks and to Stephen, begging forgiveness from his enemies, promising to join in an alliance with the Turks, and offering to seize the person of the Hungarian king. Even today this does not seem a profitable or likely course of action, and the view of Romanian historians that the letters with this plan are forgeries is probably correct. Matthias may have been embarrassed by having to explain to the Pope his tardiness in mounting a crusade at a time when Dracula came so close to success, or he may have been under pressure from the rich and influential Saxons to put their scourge out of circulation, as he had raided their towns and impaled Transylvanian citizens, but the probable reason is that Dracula was now regarded as a 'loser' and there was no benefit to the Hungarian king in having him free in Transylvania where he could plot the best means to regain his throne. This could not be to the advantage of Matthias, who had recognized Radu. With Dracula in confinement, Matthias Corvinus would be much more free to engage in the delicate diplomacy of maintaining balance between the competing powers.

Dracula's place of imprisonment is not known with certainty, although a Russian narrative says that 'he was imprisoned at Vísegràd on the Danube above Buda for twelve years'. Another theory is that he was confined in the fortress of Vàcz, which is located near Buda and also lies on the bank of the Danube. Another possibility is that Dracula could have been under 'house arrest', which would involve supervision – a more likely way of treating someone who had been a ruling prince and who, for political reasons, might once more be needed, which indeed proved to be the case.

We are fortunate to have a detailed description of Dracula by the papal legate, Nicolas Modrussa, who met him during his Hungarian captivity.

He was not very tall, but very stocky and strong, with a cold and terrible appearance, a strong and aquiline nose, swollen nostrils, a thin and reddish face in which very long eyelashes framed large wide-open green eyes; the bushy black eyebrows made them appear threatening. His face and chin were shaven, but for a moustache. The swollen temples increased the bulk of his head. A bull's neck connected his head to his body from which black curly locks hung on his wide-shouldered person.

At some stage of his detention Dracula married a kinswoman of the Hungarian king by whom he had two sons, but the condition for being allowed his freedom and so being able to marry into the royal family was that he must renounce his Orthodox faith and become a Roman Catholic. Dracula had been a builder of monasteries and was often in the company of priests of both branches of the Christian Church, so that he was not irreligious, but it is unlikely that such a worldly and ambitious man would care overmuch about a change in his religious allegiance, although it could be expected to cause grief and horror among his former subjects and the Romanians of Transylvania who had always been staunch in their allegiance to the Orthodox Church. Dracula's conversion and marriage could have taken place quite early during his detention. The Russian narrative states that these events followed 'the death of the Wallachian prince', and as Radu, the ruler recognized by

Matthias Corvinus, had died in 1475, this would mean that Dracula's marriage took place almost at the end of his official term of imprisonment, which was unlikely, as it is known that he had two sons. As the Russian story also states that Dracula lived for a short time after his Hungarian marriage, approximately ten years, and we remember that he was killed in 1476, he could have been married in 1466 and probably lived after that with his wife and family in a house in Buda.

With Dracula now safely allied to the Hungarian court, and his freedom of choice and movement limited King Matthias Corvinus was prepared to use him in a renewed Christian crusade against the Turks and appointed him a captain in the Hungarian army. The first record of a military action in which Dracula participated against the Turks is in 1474 when he was placed in charge of a Hungarian contingent which was collaborating with the Serbians. It is also possible that he took part in the great battle of Vaslui in January 1475 on the side of Stephen the Great against the Turks and the forces of the new ruler of Wallachia, Laiotă Basarab, which resulted in an important victory for Stephen.

Dracula and Stephen were now reconciled after the events of 1462. As the cornerstone of a renewed anti-Ottoman crusade sponsored by the Pope, a formal contract for mutual aid and support was signed in the summer of 1475 by Matthias, Dracula and Stephen. One of the first acts was to get Laiotă Basarab off the throne of Wallachia, where he was an ally of the Turks, and Dracula, Matthias Corvinus decided, was to be ruler in his place. On 21 January 1476 the Hungarian Diet formally gave its support to Dracula's candidacy to the Wallachian throne.

Plans were made that summer for the invasion of Wallachia. Supreme command was given to Stephen Báthory, a member of the influential Hungarian family of that name and great-uncle of the notorious Countess Elisabeth Báthory. The main reason for Báthory's command was that the bulk of his army was composed of Hungarians and Transylvanians but, Dracula was militarily in charge. There were also separate invasion forces supplied by Vuc Brancovic, the Serbian despot, and Stephen the Great.

Wallachia was attacked early in November 1476. Tîrgovişte, the capital, was captured on 8 November after a skirmish in the vicinity of the fortress, and Bucharest on 16 November. Dracula was re-established as prince of the land for the third time on 26 November but a month later he was killed in battle with the Turks who, with many of the boyars, had withdrawn to the mountains.

The boyars, knowing what had happened to members of their class at Tîrgovişte, could expect small mercy from Dracula once he had been firmly established on the throne, so that they had little reason to want him back. It may be presumed that most of Dracula's former supporters were dispersed, so that once the invasion forces had been withdrawn, except for a Moldavian bodyguard of two hundred men, the new ruler was in great danger. The final battle took place in December near Bucharest in circumstances which are obscure. Dracula's army, which comprised no more than four thousand men at most, was out-numbered, and Dracula was killed. His head was then struck from his body and sent to his old adversary in Constantinople, Mohammed II, who ordered it to be exposed in Turkish fashion for all to see that the dreaded Impaler was really dead. This must have been a cause for rejoicing at the Turkish court, but one for sorrow in western Europe, where news of Dracula's death was received about a month later.

At this stage we should pause and consider that abhorrent method of execution, impalement. According to Radu Florescu and Raymond T. McNally in their biography of Dracula,

the stakes were carefully rounded at the end and bathed in oil so that the entrails of the victims should not be pierced by a wound too fatal when the victim's legs were stretched wide apart and two horses (one attached to each leg) were sent cantering in different directions, while attendants held the stake and body firmly in place. Not all of Dracula's impalement victims were, however, pierced from the buttocks up. Judging from several prints, the men, women and children were also impaled through the heart, the naval, the stomach and the chest.

In view of the exaggerations of Saxon propagandists it is hard to assess the number of people impaled by Dracula in what was, without any doubt, a cruel age. Florescu and McNally state that 'What impresses one first is the number of victims Dracula made within the short span of a six-year rule. It ranges from a minimum of 40,000 victims to a maximum of 100,000, an estimate made by the papal nuncio, the Bishop of Erlau, near the end of Dracula's career in 1475 (this undoubtedly includes his Turkish war victims as well).'

I was fortunate in having the opportunity to discuss controversial aspects of Dracula's reigns at the Historical Institute in Bucharest, where I met Dr Dan Berindei, Vice-President of the Scientific Council of the Institute, Dr Nicolae Stoicescu, who is writing an historical monograph on Dracula, and Mr Ştefan Andreescu, studying for his doctorate, whose monograph will be on the relation between history and legends of the Impaler.

Impalement, I was told, is a very old form of execution mentioned by the Greek historian Herodotus (484–424 BC). Stephen the Great used impalement in 1467 and 1481. During the revolution of 1437 in Transylvania some peasants were impaled by Hungarian noblemen. It was the Turks who first called Dracula 'the Impaler' *(Kazaklı)*. Dracula's great enemy Mohammed II also used this method of execution and was known as *Kazaklı*. The first Romanian document which describes Vlad (Dracula) as the Impaler is dated 1551.

When considering the use of impalement we have to take into account the political and economic circumstances of the time, the historians stated. For instance, it was used as a means of protecting the Romanian merchants from the Saxons. Dracula's contemporaries considered that he used impalement as a psychological means of demonstrating his authority as at that time he had fewer forces under his command than his opponents. The Sultan who saw Turks impaled at Tîrgovişte, said 'I could never conquer a country where such methods are imposed.'

How cruel was Dracula?

Dr Berindei replied that Vlad Tepeş was always regarded by his successors as a great prince without stressing the cruel side of his nature. The Transylvanians who did not give him the money sent by the Vatican for the fight against the Turks gave his cruelty as an excuse for withholding it. Dr Berindei said that the Impaler's battles against the Turks were 'of crucial importance for Western Europe'.

According to a letter written by Stephen the Great to the Doge of Venice and kept in the archives there, all but ten of the two hundred armed men sent from Moldavia to help Dracula were killed with him. There were different stories of how Dracula met his death. One was that he was standing on a hill to watch the progress of the battle against the Turks when he was stabbed by a traitor planted in his army by the Turks, but, despite his wound, he managed to kill five of the guards who helped the traitor. This account came from Austrian chronicles but, according to a Polish source, he was killed by his relatives. Whatever the truth of these differing accounts, it was certain that he died in battle with the Turks and his head was sent to Constantinople.

Dr Berindei accepts that Dracula was buried in the monastery which he founded on the island in the lake at Snagov, twenty-five miles north of Bucharest. His final battle with the Turks was fought near there. What is believed to be his tomb was discovered in 1931 by Mr Dinu V. Rosetti, an archeologist, in front of the entrance in the church.

'Why was Vlad the Impaler's tomb placed at the entrance in the church in a spot so unfit for the rank of a ruling prince?', Rosetti asks in a magazine article.

A legend says the Impaler was buried there so that everybody should step on his tomb. I believe that those who allotted this place to him considered him unworthy of lying in the church nave according to traditions of the princely vaults on account of his sanguinary deeds. Perhaps his marrying a Roman Catholic, a kinswoman of Matthias Corvinus, may have determined the priests to deprive him of the blessings of the Greek Orthodox Church.

Dinu Rosetti admits that opinions vary as to whether this is Dracula's tomb and one of the arguments used against his theory is that a whole skeleton was found, and it is known that the Impaler's head was taken to Constantinople by the Turks. He confirms that ' I did not find a whole skeleton, only a few bones eaten away by time, and above them fragments of a silk shroud embroidered with gold and the remnants of a velvet costume with buttons of gold thread.'

Not far away was a tournament coronet. Rosetti says the argument that the grave is that of the Impaler starts from the tournament coronet and from the gold ring hidden under a button which fastened the coat in front of the heart. 'Perhaps these details might have passed unobserved if, many years later, I had not come upon a review which published an article on tournaments accompanied by a colour reproduction of the prizes awarded to the victors. They were exactly like the things discovered at Snagov.' Rosetti considers it likely that Dracula took part in tournaments. He met the obligations of noble birth and had a nature which was suited to the violence and roughness of a knightly dispute.

The present monastery at Snagov was built in 1517 on the site of Dracula's monastery and incorporates part of the old building. The approach to Snagov today is through a forest, and the area must have been heavily wooded in Dracula's time. It is difficult in summer, when people swim in the lake or sail there, to conjure up the dark days of the past when Dracula's mangled corpse was rowed to its last resting place, but to stand by the lake in winter when snow drifts on to the icy surface from leaden skies and the monastery is at times isolated is to be transported to a different scene. The plains surrounding Bucharest do not have the dramatic impact of the Transylvanian mountains, but in certain spots, such as Snagov, they retain an air of brooding mystery in winter.

When we look back on Dracula's life we realize that he lived in an era of great men – Matthias Corvinus, one of the greatest monarchs in European history, John Hunyadi, Stephen the Great and the Sultan Mohammed II. His role, compared with theirs, was comparatively minor, but obviously there was something about his personality that captured the attention of writers, as shown by the tales about him in German, Russian and Romanian, and he also became a folk hero, a protector of the weak against the strong. He was not the only impaler of his time, as we have seen, but I feel we must admit that his impalements were on such a scale that they horrified many of his contemporaries. Dracula was in many ways a complex man, devious and skilful in debate and intrigue, but a brilliant soldier and a ruthless ruler. It would be easier to understand him and his times if we knew more about him, but there are big gaps in our knowledge : for instance, we do not know the name of his mother, or, as Dr Berindei pointed out to me, who his wife was, although she was probably a cousin of the Hungarian king (the 'wife' described in legends about Poenari Citadel was a mistress). The Balkans, described as 'the cockpit of Europe' before the outbreak of the first world war, were a cockpit in Dracula's time, and his character was hardened there.

When I was reading a review of Shakespeare's *Richard III* in *Time* magazine of 4 November 1974 I came across the phrase 'Apparently, mankind's appetite for a total monster is insatiable.' Dracula has been presented to posterity as a total monster, but he was far from this, and I agree with Professors Florescu and McNally when they state in their biography of Dracula that 'The Saxon-German merchants were, in fact, responsible for besmirching Dracula's reputation throughout Europe and in the eyes of posterity.' But if the historical Dracula had not been presented as such a horrific figure Bram Stoker would never have selected him from the archives of the British Museum as the character who, transformed by his imagination, was to become a symbol of terror. It is Bram Stoker who, indirectly, has been the cause of the partial rehabilitation of Dracula's reputation in the West (I say 'partial rehabilitation' because of the horror aroused by impalement as a means of execution, just as the thought of anyone being hanged, drawn and quartered, a method of execution in England in the past, arouses horror). The spread of the Dracula cult, based on Stoker's novel and the vampire films to which it gave rise, has sent scholars and researchers to Romania, and Transylvania in particular, in search of the historical Dracula, and more will follow. As a result, the real Transylvania has been revealed, but Dracula only in part. Writers and scholars have had limited success in establishing perspective; the myth now has too strong a hold on the imagina-

tion of the masses. Indeed, as Gabriel Ronay pointed out in his
book, 'Already in the 1490s the myth was taking over from the
man.' However, I feel that as legend is stripped away from the
strange figure of Dracula his stature is not diminished but
increased. He was a prince of his times and deserved the place
assigned to him in history. But it is in legend that he continues
to fascinate and, on occasions, horrify.

4 Sighișoara, Dracula's birthplace

Dracula, or Draculea as he signed himself in later years, was probably born in 1431 in Sighișoara, the most perfectly preserved medieval town in Romania and one of the historic gems of Transylvania, with its thick walls nearly 1,000 metres long, towers, bastions, churches, cobbled streets and painted houses, crowned at the top of the hill in the citadel by a church built as a fortress.

The exact year of Dracula's birth has not been recorded, or the place, but as his father was in Sighișoara in 1430, and had a house in the citadel a year later, it is generally assumed he was born there. Mohammed II, who was to become Dracula's great adversary, was also born in 1431, it is believed.

Vlad II, or Vlad Dracul, as he is better known (very little is known about Vlad I), was, as I have mentioned before, an illegitimate son of Mircea the Old, a famous figure in Romanian history, and was one of a number of candidates for his father's throne. In 1430 he was in Sighișoara (or Schässburg, as it was known to the Saxons) as commander of the guard which watched the Transylvanian–Wallachian border. He was selected by the Hungarian king in the following year as candidate for the throne of Wallachia.

The house where Vlad Dracul lived from 1431 to 1435 in the citadel at Sighișoara near the main entrance and the clock tower is now marked by a plaque. There is nothing 'princely' about the residence; it is similar to many others probably occupied at that time by Saxon merchants. While he was in Sighișoara Dracul was given the right to mint coins which were legal tender all over Transylvania; some of these coins, which have the Order of the Dragon on one side, have survived.

Another possible link with this period are frescoes on the walls of Vlad Dracul's house. They have been covered with mortar, but in 1900 Betty Schuller, a local artist, made a copy of one fresco which showed portraits of four men. One, with a round face and moustache and dressed in a turban, could possibly be Vlad Dracul. Fresh light may be thrown on the identity of the men portrayed here when mortar is removed during the restoration of this house.

The building was used until recently as an old people's home. There were plans to convert it into an hotel and restaurant, with a beer house in the cellar, as an attraction for tourists, but the historic significance of the residence has been realized, and the indications on my last visit early in 1976 were that it would be preserved as part of the national heritage.

Sighişoara, which today has a population of 31,000, has roots that go far into the past. Bronze Age objects have been discovered on Turk's Hill near the town and to the Romans it was Castrum Sex. The first fortifications of the citadel, which rises above the town and may be seen from afar on any approach, were made of wood and earth before the Saxons came to Sighişoara in 1150. Tartars invaded the town in 1241 and burned all the wooden houses in the citadel. In 1191 only the crown of the hill was fortified, but gradually the fortifications were extended. Even so, at the end of the fourteenth century the walls were only twelve to eighteen feet high, but after the invention of gunpowder they were heightened to thirty-six feet.

In Vlad Dracul's time the citadel at Sighişoara was one of the most powerful in the country and one of the few in which the authorities had the right to punish wrongdoers by execution, according to Professor Ştefan Mosora, Director of the Museum there, to whom I am indebted for much of the information in this chapter (he is doubtful, incidentally, whether Dracula was born in the house his father occupied in the citadel as a guest of the municipality, but no one can be certain on this point).

In medieval times more than thirty craft guilds contributed to the defence of the citadel by building the three rings of walls and towers, of which nine of the original fourteen remain. All the

guilds combined to build the 200-foot-high entrance tower, later
the clock tower, in 1376, and while the richer guilds had the task
of defending a particular tower, the leader of the garrison and
his troops defended the clock tower, where four smaller towers
indicate the right to impose the death penalty.

The clock tower has always been one of the attractions of the
town. The first clock was made of wood. A local craftsman
named Kirschel installed in 1648 an ingenious mechanism by
which, at midnight, a figure over three feet tall emerged to
represent the day of the week by a sign (the moon for Monday,
Mars for Tuesday, Mercury for Wednesday, and so on) and such
figures may still be seen today. The citadel has been devastated by
three fires, and two years after the last one in 1676, which melted
the bells of the church on the hill, a new clock was installed.
Another clock, made by Devai, was installed in 1812. The
present clock was installed in 1906 by a Swiss firm.

The clock has other figures on three levels. On the first there is
a figure representing justice with a balance and near it is another
figure with one eye covered representing the law. These were put
there because the citadel was one of the few, as I have pointed
out, which had the right to pronounce the death sentence. On the
second level two figures come out of separate windows. The one
which appears at the right window at 6 am retreats into the
window at 6 pm and is replaced by a figure from the left
window which stays there until 6 am. These figures are never
seen together. On the third level the figure of a man beats the
drum at every hour. In the holiday season crowds of visitors
gather to see the drummer go into action.

When you stand on the wooden gallery which surrounds the
tower you get a fine view of the town and the houses which have
been built outside the walls since the early fifteenth century. All
seems peaceful now, with the stormy days of the past, when people
streamed into the citadel to escape from the Turks, some by the
vaulted passageway 'of the old women', long forgotten. History
predominates again when you go to the prison and the torture
chamber below the tower, where the only window has double
bars behind a small iron shutter. It is all too easy to imagine the

feelings of some poor wretch chained to the wall in this dark and damp place awaiting his turn for the rack. A few instruments of torture are still retained in the tower and others will be added when the torture chamber is opened as a museum, which could be by the time this book appears in print. The old open fire at which torture instruments were heated was partially enclosed when I visited the chamber, but it is to be restored to its former size.

One of the most valuable items in the museum in the clock tower is a book in German, printed in 1769 on the orders of Maria Theresa, Archduchess of Austria, Queen of Bohemia and Hungary, specifying which methods of torture may lawfully be applied. Among the grisly illustrations are those of torture by the thumb screw, by rope applied to the spine, by the rack and where a burning candle may be applied to the body of a prisoner on the rack. Tortures of the hands and feet are also shown. The object of this book was humanitarian, I was told; the Queen wished to avoid the use of unlawful tortures.

The clock tower, which was once the town hall, has been a museum since 1899. As you climb the wooden stairs you gain an insight into the ways of living in former days and the methods of the rulers: here are documents, old household items, musical instruments and school objects, such as a pencil holder of 1753, ceramics, weapons, icons painted on glass, old clocks and instruments for measuring time, the contents of a medieval chemist's shop, and more than 7,000 coins, some dating from Dacian times but many more minted by the Romans. Among the portraits is one of General Michael Freiherr von Melas, born in Sighişoara, who was supreme commander of the Austrian army at the battle of Marengo on 14 June 1800.

Gipsies selling copper pots and kettles circulate among visitors in the citadel, and after some brisk bargaining they can mostly be persuaded to lower the price of their wares. The gipsies are not as much in evidence now in Transylvania as in former times, although they can still make their presence felt, as when they bombarded members of the London Dracula Society with clods and other missiles after having had their photographs taken. As Boner points out in his book on Transylvania,

Like any child of nature, a gipsy is mistrustful of him who lives in a different world from himself, with wants and contrivances and tastes of which he has no idea, and which are to him unintelligible. Like the Red Indians, whose portrait Catlin painted, so the gipsy is at first afraid when you take his likeness. To him it is 'medicine' which he cannot understand. He fancies, too, [that] he loses somewhat of himself or his identity by the process. A lady artist, struck by the beauty of some children, had them fetched that they might sit to her; but they got in a great fright, and it was only by degrees they were brought to endure the penance. They never liked it, and even the money they got would hardly induce them to come. From the same cause a gipsy will sometimes cover his face when you look at him, for fear of being laid under a charm.

Charles Boner advanced the theory that the gipsies came to Transylvania in 1437, during the reign of King Sigismund, after having emigrated from India to escape the cruelty of the Mongol rulers, but one scholar told me that they were brought as slaves of the Tartars.

Indeed, this badge of slavery was still in evidence in the last century. Mrs Gerard, writing in the 1880s, said that in Wallachia 'until quite lately', gipsies were regarded as slaves or beasts of burden, 'and bought and sold like any other marketable animal.'

A Bucharest newspaper of 1845 advertised for sale two hundred gipsy families, to be disposed of in batches of five families, a handsome deduction being offered to wholesale purchasers. In Moldavia, up to 1825, a master who killed one of his own gipsies was never punished by law, but only if he killed the property of another man – the crime in that case not being considered to be murder, but merely injury to another man's property.

In Hungary alone these wanderers found themselves neither oppressed nor repulsed, 'and if the gipsy can be said to feel at home anywhere on the face of the globe, it is surely here', Mrs Gerard said. In the 1880s there were more than 150,000 gipsies in Hungary, 'of which about 80,000 fall to the share of Transylvania, which therefore in still more special degree may be termed the land of gipsies.'

Transylvania was still very much a land of the gipsies in 1929, when Dr Walter Starkie wandered among them with his fiddle, but much of the old way of life was swept away in the holocaust of the second world war, and today there are only a few thousand gipsies in the whole of Romania. Twenty years ago they were compelled by law to settle.

The church of the former Dominican monastery near the clock tower, built in Gothic style in the thirteenth century, contains a valuable collection of Oriental carpets. Such carpets were gifts by Saxon merchants returning from their travels in the Middle East and Boner found these carpets in almost every church in Transylvania; by this I take it to mean almost every Saxon church, because the Romanians of that time and earlier periods did not have the same privileges as the Saxons.

There is a particularly fine collection of Oriental carpets in the Black Church in Braşov. Mrs Gerard, who admired, as I did, these carpets, passed through Sighişoara when travelling to Braşov, and declared it to be the prettiest of the Saxon towns on the route. 'Towers and ramparts peep out tantalisingly from luxurious vegetation, making us long to get out and explore the place; particularly inviting is a steep flight of steps leading to an old church at the top of a hill ', she wrote.

Charles Boner, unlike Mrs Gerard, did have time to explore Sighişoara, and the old town moved him to indulge in passages of purple prose: 'No place in Transylvania so fixes your attention by its exquisite picturesqueness, nor as you look from the upper town down into the vales, can you remember to have seen a spot that has such a charm and such amenity.'

In his chapter on Schässburg (Sighişoara) Boner says that

Pompeii, locked up in lava, has supplied us with something far better than written history. We have bodily before us a piece of a long-past century – real, palpable; and, though lifeless, still here are the actors – each just as he was suddenly arrested in the very midst of action.

Now, in Transylvania, we have something akin to this. Here, too, is a people that had strayed to the land beyond the forest, and sat there for centuries, locked out from intercourse with their kind.

Not, of course, like men wrecked on an island in some lonely sea; but apart from that communion with their fellows, without which, in Europe, men become like bees in amber, and when chanced upon are, to the finder, as interesting as fossil remains. Indeed, they have something of their value and character; for they furnish what nothing else could give, and they indicate a state that is most curious, because gone from us for ever.

Charles Boner is referring here, of course, to the Saxon settlers, who,

preserved all their old ways unchanged for centuries, as though their very existence depended on doing so. For them the world had all that while been standing still. . . . Words elsewhere forgotten are in daily use here. Forms and ceremonials that we read of as half-mythical observances constitute a part of everyday life. The Saxon peasant tills his fields now just as he did when the wild hordes used to desolate them. He is still distrustful, forgetting that in five hundred years much has changed, that there is no *voivode* to call on him for levies, that no cry will be raised to shut the town gates for safety against the advancing Turk.

Although Boner's book was published more than a century ago, and Sighişoara is now more of a Romanian town than a Saxon one, the passages I have quoted do suggest the feeling of timelessness which still persists here.

It was in Sighişoara, too, that Boner was moved to protest about unpunctuality (I have found that present-day Romanians do keep appointments on time).

On leaving Schässburg I had to wait a long time before my waggon was ready; and it was suggested to me that the driver was possibly waiting till the clock had struck twelve, as throughout Transylvania there is a superstition that to start on a journey between eleven and noon is unlucky. Whether there is also a superstition about making haste and keeping time I do not know, but in my life I never met such want of punctuality as here. I always thought that in this respect Bavarians were bad enough, and were not to be surpassed. Of all wares, time with them is the cheapest. But in this country absolutely *no one* kept to time. For a person you had ordered punctually at seven to make his appearance at nine was not thought extraordinary. Punctuality is simply a thing unknown.

Boner wrote about shutting the town gates for safety against the advancing Turk, but they were also shut for safety in internal wars, such as in the dispute about the throne of Hungary between John Zápolya, Governor of Transylvania, and the Emperor Ferdinand of Austria, following the disastrous defeat of the Hungarian forces by the Turkish army in the battle of Mohács in 1526. Zápolya had the support of the Hungarian nobles but the Saxons favoured the Emperor. In the course of the struggle the Governor of Transylvania, Stephen Báthory, laid siege to Sighişoara. The suburbs and a great part of the lower town were burnt, but the upper fortress could not be taken.

Before this, Boner points out, the citadel was on the point of going to ruin from being deserted by the inhabitants. The place was already solitary, and King Ladislas began to fear that the land would lose one of the firmest bulwarks against the invasions of Turks and Tartars.

With wisdom and forethought, he ordered that all those trades which, according to olden custom, had till now been carried on in the Burgh, were henceforth to return and not settle elsewhere; and moreover, that all wares were to be exposed for sale there, and there only. Whoever built a new house in the Burgh was to be tax-free for seven years. And later, the magistrates and town council ordained that in future the court of justice should be held only in the citadel; that the half of the councilmen and of the four principal guilds – tailors, goldsmiths, locksmiths and carpenters – might dwell there and nowhere else. By these regulations, the upper town was again inhabited and preserved.

The citadel was also twice captured by the Szeklers.

The 'steep flight of steps' referred to by Mrs Gerard are obviously the 175 covered steps built in 1642 leading to the church on the hill, which was started in 1345 and, with extensions, finished in the second half of the fifteenth century, and the schools below it. The cover is a useful protection against ice. On one late winter visit I saw the pupils skidding skilfully from door to door, but I went sprawling. I had climbed the hill to gain a prospect of the towers, on which the patina of age on the red tiles contrasted with patches of newly-fallen snow, and the town.

Most of the houses in the citadel date from the seventeenth century, but, as with Vlad Dracul's house, some are earlier. One, dating from the thirteenth century, has been partly modernized when old doors and windows deteriorated. The house has two small windows at the top from which a family in former times could fire at their attackers: fortified churches, farms and houses bear witness to Transylvania's stormy history. Today all is quiet in the citadel, protected by its height from the floods which can ravage the lower part of the town. In 1971 and 1975 water from the flooded river Tîrnava reached the first floor of houses in the main street.

Most of my inquiries in Sighişoara were about the history of the town, and I had little time to inquire about folk beliefs, but even a casual inquiry brings accounts of customs peculiar to a particular locality to light. For instance, I was told by an official at the local tourist office that after a wedding in the villages of Sîncel, Biia, St Nicolae, Cetatea de Baltă and Spini surrounding the town of Blaj, north of Sibiu, the family and guests, preceded by horsemen, walked to the bride's home, where a horse has to kick open the gate to allow the party to enter. By local custom, however, members of the bride's family and neighbours group round the gate to prevent the horse from getting near it. After a while resistance stops, the horse is backed to the gate to kick it open with its hoofs, and the wedding party enters. On the following day the feast is continued at the home of the bridegroom.

Sighişoara makes its own most distinctive contribution to folk legend in a story of what can only be called an enchanted tower. This is Catherine's Tower outside the town. 'It is a tower of no historical significance and can only be explained by legend', Professor Dr Vasile Drăguţ, Director of the Department of Historic and Art Monuments, told me in Bucharest. The legend, he said, was that a Turkish pasha riding a white elephant was buried there, and if you climbed the tower and looked through a small hole you could still see the pasha on his elephant.

'Restoration revealed no hole in the tower,' said Dr Drăguţ.
'Under pressure of local belief we dug beneath the tower but
found no grave. There is no reasonable explanation for the
tower.'

Mrs Gerard saw the 'solitary turret perched on the over-
hanging cliff above the river' during her brief stop in Sighişoara,
and, on inquiring, was told that it was said to mark the place
where a Turkish pasha, besieging the town with his army, was
slain by a shot fired from the goldsmiths' tower. The pasha was
buried there sitting on his elephant, and this tower raised above
them, while that other tower from whence the shot was fired,
held ever since in high honour, was decked out with a golden
ceiling.

Mrs Gerard remarked that ' Why the elephant was also buried
is not very apparent, as it is hardly to be supposed that it was
killed by the same shot which slew the pasha.' As Dr Drăguţ has
pointed out, however, the pasha is not buried under the tower,
nor, one may assume, is his elephant, so that the tower ' can only
be explained by legend '.

Boner gives few examples of folk beliefs in his book, but one is
that in Neudorf, near Sighişoara (the name of the village is now
Noul Săsesc), there is a prevalent superstition that at midnight on
New Year's night the cattle speak, but in a language which man
may not hear; if he does, he dies.

When Boner was travelling to Transylvania his driver pointed
out to him a point in the mountains where one evening he had
seen 'a gold fire', and explained that this was a light which
hovers over the spot where gold was buried. Later he searched
for the treasure, but as the light was seen from a distance he
could not find the exact spot and therefore got nothing. The
belief that light indicates hidden treasure may be found in a
country as remote from Transylvania as Peru.

I wish that time had permitted me to search for accounts of
folk beliefs in Sighişoara because undoubtedly they exist. When
Boner was there he made contact with the branch society of the
association for promoting knowledge of all relating to Transylvania. One of its leading members, Rector Frederic Müller, had

published a book on Transylvanian traditions, 'A rich accumu-
lation of stories originating in, and throwing a light upon popular
belief', and one of the famous Grimm brothers corresponded
with a professor at Sighişoara, 'delighted with the rich collection
this gentleman was making in folklore, and urging him to
proceed. As there is a gymnasium at Schässburg, youths come
thither from all parts; and from their lips the old stories, nursery
rhymes, charms and fairy tales were written down as they
repeated them.'

A romantic but tragic story, with more than a hint of puzzle
in it, attaches to Sighişoara, because it was near here at Albeşti
that Sándor Petöfi, one of Hungary's greatest poets, whose works
have been translated into more than fifty languages, met his
death at the age of twenty-six in the Battle of Schässburg on 31
July 1849, when the Hungarians in revolt, led by the Polish
General Bem, were crushed by the superior numbers of the
Russian troops who came to Austria's assistance.

Mrs Gerard said that 'Petöfi's body was never found, nor had
anyone seen him fall, and for many years periodical reports got
afloat in Hungary that the great poet was not dead, but pining
away his life in the mines of Siberia. There seems, however, to be
no valid reason for believing this tale, and more likely his was
one of the many mutilated and unrecognizable corpses which
strewed the valley of Schässburg on that disastrous day.'

What was Petöfi, who was born on the Hungarian steppe,
doing in Transylvania? He travelled the country as an itinerant
actor and was caught up in the revolutionary fervour which
resulted in the 1848 uprising. And he fell in love, gaining as a
wife Julia Szendrey, 'the princess of Ardud' (a centre south of
Satu Mare in north-western Transylvania near the border with
Hungary), whom he conquered in spite of her father's stubborn
resistance: he looked down on the dishevelled and destitute
young man. Petöfi took her as 'the wife among wives' to the
manor in Coltău, northern Transylvania, of his friend Sándor
Teleki, who was also the friend of Liszt and Victor Hugo and
was known as 'the wild count'. The young poet participated in
the main battles in the 1848-9 revolution. He spent the last night

of his life at Cristuru Secuiesc, near the scene of the final battle, writing a poem under a pear tree which, according to one Romanian writer, 'defying time, still gets covered with green leaves today'. Such is Petöfi's fame that there are statues, monuments, memorial plaques, museums, or memorial houses at places where he stayed or fought in Transylvania, and to Hungarians at least Sighişoara is better known as the town near where Petöfi met his death than as the birthplace of Dracula.

In 1976 Sighişoara celebrated the 600th anniversary of the reorganization of the guilds (they were established before this, but earlier documents are lacking), and in 1980 more celebrations will mark the 700th anniversary of the first document (dated 1280) which gave the name of the upper citadel as Castrum Sex. The renovation of the clock tower and other towers in the citadel is now in progress with the goal that in 1980 exhibitions of the activities of the guilds concerned may be held in these towers. For tourists from Western and Far Eastern countries, however, the point of greatest interest in the town will undoubtedly be Vlad Dracul's house when it is restored.

Sighişoara does not seem to come into the Dracula saga again. It was spared the raids which the Impaler made, when Prince of Wallachia, on other Saxon trading towns such as Braşov and Sibiu. Possibly this was because Sighişoara was not of sufficient commercial importance. The fact that the town was his birthplace was unlikely to have deterred him. Dracula was the least sentimental of men. Sighişoara has now awakened from the sleep of centuries mentioned by Boner. Whenever I am there I get the impression of a dozy market town, but it has a range of industrial units: leather goods, ready-made clothes, food and a modern faience and glass combine on the road leading to Albeşti, where supposedly Petöfi fell and was never found.

5 Dracula's castle and the punishment of the boyars

Dracula's Castle, or Poenari Citadel to give it the correct name, is today a ruin that stands on a crag 1,200 feet above the road and is approached by 1,440 steps, which may account for the fact that only a small proportion of pilgrims on Dracula tours care to make the climb. At night floodlights throw the citadel into relief against the surrounding darkness of sky and hill, but when I toiled up the steps in August 1974 the sun was shining and it was possible to see in the concrete the prints of such animals as the bear, lynx, deer and fox left at night when the steps were being constructed three years earlier following the partial restoration of the citadel.

We are now in Wallachia, north of the old princely capital of Curtea de Argeş, but not far from the Transylvanian border. The first impression you get of the citadel is how small it is, but this is understandable : a third of the castle collapsed in 1888 and rolled down the mountainside. You enter the citadel by a narrow wooden bridge and find inside remnants of two of the five original towers, the central tower being in the form of a prism. The thick walls have been restored. I suspect that, but for the developing Dracula industry, this inaccessible ruin would have been allowed to crumble into further decay. Bram Stoker would never have chosen this place as the home of his fictional Count Dracula – Bran Castle or Hunedoara Castle would have been much more suitable for his purposes.

Poenari Citadel is, in the true sense of the word, an eyrie. When you stand on the battlements you gaze out at the wooded lower foothills of the Făgăraş range and over the Argeş Valley through which the river of that name winds. The date when this citadel was built is unknown. It is excellently sited from a

strategic viewpoint, commanding, as it does, the road through
the gorge below from Curtea de Argeş to the town of Făgăraş,
which, between the fourteenth century and the late fifteenth
century, was a fief of Wallachia. In 1330 a battle was fought
between the forces of Basarab i, ruler of Wallachia, and those
of the Hungarian king, Carol (or Charles) Robert, in the vicinity
of the citadel, which was then known as Castrum Argyas. The
Hungarian monarch and his army were apparently caught in a
neatly laid ambush in the gorge below the castle, being pinned
down by arrows fired from the battlements and crushed by
boulders tumbled down from the heights above. In four days
the Hungarians were destroyed.

When Dracula was on the throne of Wallachia the citadel was
in ruins, and nothing better illustrates his ruthlessness than the
manner in which he had it restored. I have already referred to
the impalement of the boyars outside Tîrgovişte. They were
seized during a banquet, but only the older men and their wives
were put to death. The younger ones, their wives and children
were forced to march to the Argeş Valley to work on the
restoration of the citadel.

The reasons for Dracula's drastic action against the boyars
have always been obscure. Most probably Dracula punished the
boyars for their support of his brother Mircea, who wanted the
throne. As the throne was not then vacant – Mircea and his
father were killed after losing a battle – this action by Dracula
seemed to me to be unduly harsh, but this was an age in which
dynastic feuds were frequent, and Dracula was always ruthless
when he felt his claim to a throne was threatened. The story of
the seizure of the boyars was attested in official documents
(Romanian) of the sixteenth century.

The trek from Tîrgovişte to Poenari must have been long and
painful. We do not know how many men, women and children,
clad in their Easter finery, took part in it or how many perished
on the way. Within the villages surrounding the castle site
Dracula had given orders for brick ovens and lime kilns to be
built. The survivors of the trek who had arrived exhausted were
now formed into what was virtually a slave gang. While some

made bricks others passed materials from hand to hand up the steep mountainside. Local tradition has it that the young boyars and their families worked until their clothes were in shreds and some were naked. Many must have died from sheer exhaustion. It would be surprising if there were many survivors when the castle was eventually rebuilt.

Visitors to Poenari Citadel will be told the story, as I was, of how Dracula, in the days before he passed into Hungarian captivity, was besieged there by the Turks and made a dramatic escape. Dracula's situation seemed hopeless. With the remnants of his army he was holed up in his castle, which had been bombarded by Turks with cherry wood cannons but without success owing to the thickness of the walls. The orders for the final assault were to have been given the following day, but during the night a Romanian who was a member of the janissary corps climbed a commanding height and sent by arrow a message warning Dracula that he must escape while there was yet time. He had aimed at a candle in an opening of the tower that contained Dracula's living quarters. The candle was suddenly extinguished. When it was relit Dracula's wife could be seen reading the message. She told her husband that she would ' rather have her body rot and be eaten by the fish of the Argeş than be led into captivity by the Turks'. After this she flung herself into the river below. Dracula, however, thought there was a slender chance of escape. He followed his scouts through a secret passage leading to the banks of the river and there, invoking the aid of local peasants, made his way over the mountains to Transylvania and safety.

Dracula is said to have been guided to safety by five peasants from Aref, the village below the citadel, and before parting from them asked how best he could reward them for saving his life. They refused money but accepted land, which would be quite in character with peasant values. Dracula then offered them all the area to the south as far as they could see up the plain, containing sixteen mountains and rich grazing land, as well as rivers filled with fish. He confirmed his gift in writing but not on paper; he used the skin of hares caught the previous day. There is an old tradition in Aref that these skins are still in existence, hidden carefully by the descendants of the families thus endowed.

I asked Dr Berindei his opinion of this story of Dracula's escape from Poenari Citadel and he dismissed it as legend. He believed that there was no truth in the story that the citadel was besieged by Turks or that Dracula's 'wife' threw herself to her death from the battlements. It was not known how many wives or concubines he had. The identity of the woman with whom he was living then was not known, but she was not his wife. She was pregnant at the time and did not kill herself. Dracula had a son, Michael, by a woman to whom he was not married, but under the laws of that time he was entitled to succeed him (as I have stated earlier, the only woman accepted as Dracula's wife was the kinswoman of the Hungarian king, but even her name is not known. Dr Berindei told me that a letter of 11 February 1462 from Dracula to King Matthias Corvinus told him that the Turks were putting pressure on him not to marry this woman because it would endanger the alliance between him and the Turks).

Dr Berindei thought the story that Dracula had given the five villagers of Aref and their descendants the land on sixteen mountains was a legend which had grown out of an old tradition in which peasants who had worked for the owners of the citadel had acquired the land.

A believer in the truth of the story of Dracula's gift of land to the villagers is the priest of Aref, Ion Stan Stănciulescu, a brisk, grey-haired man with a small beard and a local historian. He has been *popa* of the village for forty-six years and was born there, as were his father and grandfather before him. He assured me that it was his love of the people and of folklore that made him stay there.

Here was a golden opportunity to find out on the spot what memories of Dracula persisted in a village which he must often have visited, as he must also have visited Căpăţînenii Pămînteni, a village just across the river, where there is a statue of Dracula. The *popa* said that his father, who had died a few years ago at the age of ninety-two, had carried out some research on Dracula, and according to him and to old legends, the Impaler was 'an exceedingly good-hearted Prince' in his dealings with the ordinary people, but very severe with traitors and those who tried to take away the belongings of his subjects; he impaled them. The *popa* thought that Dracula's use of this form of execution was influenced by Turkish practice.

Aref is a long, rambling, ramshackle village, with a population of 2,000, and can easily be missed as you drive along the main road. The village has some old wooden houses and other rather crudely-built modern ones of brick (house building in eastern European countries is often a co-operative one by the family concerned, relatives, friends and neighbours). Turkeys and geese scuttled to safety as our car bumped along the rough track leading to the village square, passing two horses with red tassels dangling from their harness pulling a cart filled with logs. Wayside shrines showed the influence of religion in the village. My interview with the priest took place in the council offices, and while I waited for the priest to arrive I watched well-dressed children from the kindergarten performing exercises in a circle with a little one in the centre as leader.

The *popa* came with a monograph on which he has been working for forty years and many documents relating to the history of the village which, according to tradition, had existed since 300 BC, although the first documents referring to it were dated 1546. There was a theory that the first prince of the region, Litovoi, had his court at Aref and after that moved to Curtea de Argeş. The village had been known successively as Hareş, Haref, and since 1832 Aref, because it was easier to pronounce. The residents worked at animal breeding and forestry. Many of the young people were engaged in industry: there are extensive hydro-electric works in the neighbourhood.

The *popa* produced a copy of the document signed by Prince Mircea in 1546 in which he said he was prince of the Romanian countries by right of inheritance. According to all the documents he had read, the village belonged rightfully to the villagers of Hareş (now Aref), and he restated the right of the villagers to the ownership of these territories, which included sixteen mountains. Another document, issued by Prince Radu in 1606, stated that he had checked the rights of ownership issued by three former reigning princes – one was Laiotă Basarab, a contemporary of Dracula – and he reaffirmed them.

The villagers of Aref kept the ownership of these territories until 1804, when the boyars tried to take it away from them. A long legal action started and it did not end until 1908. As a result, the villagers retained only 4,500 hectares of the 20,000 hectares that had been in dispute.

The *popa* said he thought that Poenari Citadel was built by one of Dracula's predecessors, although there was a theory that it was constructed by Teutonic knights who tried to convert the inhabitants of these territories to Roman Catholicism. He discounted stories that peasants had a superstitious fear of the castle. I could not see why they should be afraid of Dracula's eyrie if he was regarded, as he obviously is, as a local benefactor. I was not aware of any sinister atmosphere when I stood in the citadel, with ravens circling under the blue sky and the silence only broken by the indistinct call of an animal from the woods on the opposite hillside. But, so steep was the approach, I could not help feeling sympathy with the wretched boyars who had been forced to rebuild the Impaler's fortress.

I asked the *popa* if there was still a belief among the villagers in ghosts and the evil eye? He knew nothing about the existence of such beliefs now, but there was a reference to them in documents dated 1832, although these did not give accounts of actual experiences.

This was rather discouraging, but the *popa* warmed as he described the religious festivities at Christmas. Only in this village, he said, were there variations of the traditional Christmas carol depending on the house before which it was sung. For the priest the carol stressed the religious nature of the occasion and the faith of the people in God and religion; for a house in which there was an old person, good wishes and respect for the old; but for a house where there were girls the verses were humorous.

I was reminded here of a passage in Peter Neagoe's novel of Transylvanian life, *Easter Sun,* in which he said that

On Christmas Day, from early morning until evening, the boys would go from house to house to perform 'Herod and the Magi'. They were paid, or rather rewarded, with sausages, pieces of cheese, a slice of smoked ham or bacon, a corner of spiced bread and even with eggs – the Shepherd, being the humblest, carried the bag and would ask timidly, 'Are they boiled, the eggs?' For if they were not, he would have to put them in his shirtbosom, and that was embarrassing, to say the least.

Neagoe's account of Christmas carolling is confirmed by Marcu Beza in his *Paganism in Roumanian Folklore*. He says that on Christmas Eve small bands of boys go from house to house singing carols which bear the special name of *colinde*. Composed largely in blank verse, these carols are of much interest, not only because of their peculiar blending of Pagan and Christian ideas, but likewise for allusions they contain to the life and circumstances of yore. The most familiar is the one beginning:

> Tonight, great night,
>> White flowers!
> The great night of Christmas,
>> White flowers!

Or, says Mr Beza, that given by V. Alecsandri in his *Folk Poems*:

> Arise, great boyars, arise,
>> White flowers! ...

Their singing ends up with a loud, hearty greeting by the whole band: 'Good morning to the old Christmas!' Upon which they ask, and are given, beside fruit or money, a kind of home-made cake.

I was told that Christmas carolling is still carried out by parties of boys in Transylvania and other parts of Romania. Fifty years ago Dr Starkie wrote of the Romanians' attachment to their Orthodox religion and, despite changing times, this attachment is still very much in evidence today.

As we left Aref I paused to look once more at Poenari Citadel. Archeologists have estimated that it could not hold more than 160 people. If we accept the story of Dracula's escape as related by the villagers, a force of this size, if accompanied by horses, could not go down such a steep hillside at night without making a great clatter. If, on the other hand, a secret passage was used, where were the remains of it? The passage could, of course, have collapsed during an earthquake, but in such a small castle excavations should be able to locate the former opening of the passage, if ever it existed. As I have said earlier, Dr Berindei dismisses as legend the story of the siege of the castle by Turks and Dracula's escape.

If Dracula could be transported bodily to the present day he would have to take care, in descending from his eyrie, to avoid the electrified cables at the foot of the hill, where the only evidence of the important Gheorghe Gheorghiu-Dej hydro-electric power station below is an administrative pavilion and a water tower over 400 feet high. The four underground turbines have an installed power of 200,000 kilowatts and an annual production of 400 million kilowatts. These turbines are supplied with water coming from the Vidraru storage lake above. Here, as at Tîrgovişte and Hunedoara, is evidence of the blending of old and new in Romania, but despite the introduction of technology to the Argeş valley, the area still conveys an impression of aridity.

Before I left Bucharest Dr Bărbulescu had told me that the Argeş region was poorly represented in the collection of folk beliefs held in his Institute, and I can quite believe that this is so. I had hopes of coming across some material in the village of Retevoieşti, on the road from Curtea de Argeş to Cîmpulung, as it contains a museum in a *cula* (two-storeyed fortified house) with historical and ethnographical exhibits, but the museum was closed, and the curator, Vasile Popescu, whom we found in his home, could not help us to any extent. He said there was an old belief that those who died without confession would be changed into *strigoii* and an unbaptized child would also become a ghost after death, and do harm to those he loved, but beliefs such as this are not held today, and only one or two very old women still believed that illnesses could be cured by magical means.

There was snow on the ground, and Mr Popescu, who has lived in the village for more than forty years, received us in his kitchen so that we would be warm. In 1716, he said, the Black Death struck this village and only a dozen people remained alive. Since then it has been repopulated by people from Oltenia in western Wallachia (an area, incidentally, rich in folk beliefs), and today there are 2,800 inhabitants of the village.

Mr Popescu is a native of Bessarabia, an area of Moldavia and northern Bukovina that is now in Soviet hands, although the population is predominantly Romanian. It has long been an issue between the two countries. The whole area became part of Romanian Moldavia in the fifteenth century. Princes of Moldavia sought Russian support in their struggle with the invading Turks, and the Russians later brought it under their control, but the Bessarabians voted for union with Romania in 1918, and this union was recognized by the Treaty of Paris in 1920, although the Russians never admitted Romania's right to the province. In 1940, after the collapse of the Western Front against Hitler, a Soviet ultimatum was issued to Romania demanding the cession of Bessarabia and of northern Bukovina 'as compensation for Romanian misrule in Bessarabia'. The Romanians had to submit, but in July 1941 Romania, having entered the war as Germany's ally against the USSR, reoccupied Bessarabia. The tables were turned again in 1944, although the Russians and Romanians had then become allies, and Bessarabia was once again in Soviet hands.

Some recent maps of Romania have Bessarabia and northern Bukovina in a shaded portion, but this, I gather, is to show them as historical Romanian territories and is not meant to imply a claim for them. There is little the Romanians can do about the Bessarabians who have been exiled to remote parts of the Soviet Union for their nationalist sentiments, but by showing awareness of the disputed status of Bessarabia they can do something to divert the Russians from their implied support of Hungarian nationalism in Transylvania which is engendered more by emigrés than by the Hungarian government.

My excursion to Retevoieşti was made during a return trip to Curtea de Argeş (the name means the Court of Argeş), a quiet little town of 20,000 people which is rich in memories of Dracula and his forebears. Dracula's grandfather, Mircea the Old, had his court here, as did his father, Vlad Dracul, at times. Dracula stayed here as a child and must have visited it often as an adult, although his court was at Tîrgovişte and Bucharest.

In Curtea de Argeş, as in the citadel at Sighişoara, one gets the impression that time has stood still. There is a certain amount of controversy about whether Cîmpulung or Curtea de Argeş was the first true capital of Wallachia, but the indications are that the first *voivodes,* Seneslau and Tihomir, lived here in the second half of the thirteenth century, so that the honour should, perhaps, go to Curtea de Argeş. Basarab I, generally regarded as the founder of Wallachia, was the son of Tihomir and had his capital in Cîmpulung in 1330. In 1369, however, the court was once again established in Curtea de Argeş and this is the year in which the first documents were issued from the princely residence. The term 'princely residence' gives an impression of grandeur, but when you visit the ruins of the court you realize how small that court must have been. Although nothing but ruins enclosed by thick walls made of river boulders remain of the court, the fine princely church, begun by Basarab I in the middle of the fourteenth century, still stands. It was a very chilly place indeed when I visited it in February 1976, and was relieved to be assured by the curator that I could keep my hat on if I wished, as the building was no longer a church but a museum.

My hands were so cold that I could scarcely write, but this church, which stands on the site of one built in 1250, is well worth a visit because it contains the oldest wall paintings in Romania, dating from 1384. They were revealed during restoration work in 1914. In the course of time the building has undergone change, but it was restored, to a fair extent, to its original shape between 1911 and 1929. During this restoration graves of former princes and noblemen and the ruins of the princely court were revealed. The cupola of the church, which has sixteen long niches, is regarded as the most representative Wallachian dome of the period.

For every person who visits the princely church at Curtea de Argeş one hundred or more flock to the famous episcopal church, or monastery, as it is better known there, regarded by many as the most beautiful church in Romania. It is certainly among the more important architectural monuments in Europe. Guide books and tourist literature state that this monastery was founded by ruling prince Neagoe Basarab between 1512 and 1515, but according to Dr Vasile Drăguț, Director of the Department of Historic and Art Monuments, whom I interviewed in Bucharest, recent research has indicated that the builder was the Impaler's father. This was indeed a surprise to me and will be to the countless guides who have pointed out the tombs of Neagoe Basarab, his wife Despina, and of their four children in the monastery with the remark that how fitting it is that the 'founder' should have his last resting place here. Vlad Dracul and his son built many churches. Dracula, who must have watched the construction of this monastery, is buried at Snagov, a monastery with which he was intimately connected, as we have seen, and he was certainly the founder of the church of St Nicholas at Tîrgșor, near Ploiești, in 1461, but his father's burial place is not known, although renewed interest in Dracula may bring this information to light.

The monastery, set in a charming park, was extensively damaged by fire and neglected over the centuries, but extensive repairs were begun in 1875 under the direction of the French architect André Lacomte de Nouy and took eleven years to complete. When you are in the monastery you get the same feeling of being in a national monument as you do in St Paul's Cathedral in London, or the Cathedral of Nôtre Dame in Paris, although both are places where services are held regularly. I was once in Curtea de Argeș on a saint's day, and a church near the monastery was thronged with worshippers, mainly women. The Orthodox religion is well supported by the population, although, as in other countries, the numbers of those who attend services are much less than before. I have also visited, although often briefly, well-attended church services in other East European countries, usually in rural areas, but against this must be recorded the fact that numbers of old and historic churches are preserved as historic monuments rather than as places of worship.

The Romanians, it seems to me, have a genius for combining the sacred and secular, so that in a peasant's cottage you may find a collection of President Ceauşescu's works in handsome volumes in a room which also contains icons.

The monastery at Curtea de Argeş, a guide once pointed out to me, is a target for all the romantics in Romania because of the legend attached to it of the master builder Manole, who is said to have immured his wife in the walls because they kept crumbling. On the completion of the work Manole was sacrificed by the ruling prince lest he should build another edifice of equal beauty. This prince caused the scaffolding to be removed from the building while the master builder was still on the roof, but Manole, with the help of wings made from shingles, tried to float to earth. He crashed, and on the spot where he fell a spring gushed out. You can drink today from Manole's well near the monastery.

In any legend there is probably a vestige of truth, and it is probable that the builder of the monastery experienced difficulties during construction. This belief is not based merely on supposition. Dr Drăguţ told me there was a legend that the monastery was built on a ruin and recent excavations have proved that this is true. Investigation of so-called haunted houses in England has indicated at times that cracks in walls, subsidence, doors that open by themselves and unexplained noises occur when a building stands on an insecure foundation such as the remains of a former dwelling. The builders of the monastery, puzzled by difficulties during construction and fearing the wrath of the ruling prince who wanted his piety to be recognized by his contemporaries and by posterity, *may* have caused a living person to be immured in the walls or foundation. In *The Golden Bough* Sir James Frazer speaks of 'the old practice of immuring a living person in the walls, or crushing him under the foundations of a new building, in order to give strength and durability to the structure, or more definitely in order that the angry ghost may haunt the place and guard it against the intrusion of enemies.'

A later development of this practice was that of walling in the shadow of a person instead of the body. In his famous book, which was first published in 1890, Frazer pointed out that perhaps nowhere does the equivalence of the shadow to the life or soul come out more clearly than in some customs 'practised to this day' in south-eastern Europe (Dr Bărbulescu told me that this is a belief of the past and 'today is lost').

Frazer said that

The Roumanians of Transylvania think that he whose shadow is thus immured will die within forty days; so persons passing by a building which is in course of erection may hear a warning cry, 'Beware, lest they take thy shadow!' Not long ago there were still shadow-traders whose business it was to provide architects with the shadows necessary for securing their walls. In these cases the measure of the shadow is looked on as equivalent to the shadow itself, and to bury it is to bury the life or soul of the man, who, deprived of it, must die.

We return briefly now from Wallachia to Transylvania to visit Bran Castle, a fortress built on a rock. It was used in the Middle Ages to protect the Giuvala Pass, a trade route between Wallachia and Transylvania, and was among John Hunyadi's castles. This castle, which is included in the itinerary of Dracula and other conducted tours, is thought by many visitors to be one of Dracula's castles, but this is not so. He certainly stayed here as a guest, however, as did his father before him, and the castle may therefore be included in 'Dracula Country'.

Before the Prahova Valley in the southern Carpathians became the usual communication line between Wallachia and Transylvania, the Bran road, which was drawn as early as the fourth century on the map of the Roman Empire, was the main link between the two Romanian provinces. The first fortress to be built here was at the orders of a knight of the Teutonic Order named Dietrich (it will be remembered that some think that Poenari Castle was built by Teutonic knights). Andrew II of Hungary had settled these knights in Transylvania as colonists in 1211, but fourteen years later they were expelled to Poland because of their expansionist tendencies. In 1377 the citizens of Braşov, only fifteen miles away, built a new citadel here to protect the access to their town.

D

A well 174 feet deep provided water during the many sieges to which the castle was subjected and is said to be connected to a secret passage. In former times prisoners in the dungeons must have been kept in near darkness as the only light came from one small window cut in the wall above the precipice.

This imposing castle, surrounded by woods, was turned into an interesting museum of feudal art in 1957. The museum on the first floor has five rooms full of furniture in the Renaissance style and gives access to the dungeons. On the next floor, which was occupied by the owners of the castle, the furniture is baroque. The third floor opens on to a terrace and hall with a fine view of the inner courtyard, one of my favourite spots there. The fourth and last floor is a wide terrace bordered by a wall from where you admire the spreading valley and stream below. Bran Castle has always impressed me as being a noble residence in the European tradition such as you could find in a number of countries, including England, Scotland and Wales. It is easy to imagine soldiers pouring out of the castle in times of war to take control of the strategic roads. Possibly Bram Stoker, poring over old maps and illustrations in the British Museum, came upon a picture of Bran Castle and transported it in print to western Transylvania far from the Wallachian border. But it is not necessary to strain after links with fiction when placing Dracula as an historical character in the setting of Bran Castle and its environs. He must have passed this way many times in his journeys between Transylvania and Wallachia, not to mention on his raiding expeditions.

Wallachia did not give me the accounts of folk beliefs I had hoped to find there, but I had made my search in only a small portion of it and would have had more success in, say, Oltenia, if time had allowed. There is little doubt, however, that of the three provinces comprising modern Romania, Transylvania contains the richest store of remaining folk beliefs. An indication of this is the many references to Transylvanian folk beliefs in *The Golden Bough,* but, as I indicated earlier, modern Romanian scholars think that Frazer relied too heavily on literary sources for his material. They regard oral tradition as more reliable. It is significant that the archives of folk institutes throughout the world now contain taped accounts of folk beliefs; this lessens the chances of misunderstanding what the narrator said or of misinterpreting it.

From time to time in this book I have mused on possible origins of the fictional Count Dracula's castle. Poenari Citadel may be ruled out – I doubt if Bram Stoker ever heard of it – but Bran Castle and Hunedoara Castle are possible sources of inspiration, although far from the Bîrgău Pass. On reflection, I feel that Jules Verne's *The Castle of the Carpathians* could have influenced Stoker. In both novels the castle described has a dream-like quality and, as Verne's book was published only four years before *Dracula,* and as Stoker at that time was seeking material (Verne had been to Transylvania and he had not), what is more likely than that he should turn to it?

In Jules Verne's novel the castle

Did not stand out in relief from the background of mountains. What might have been taken as a donjon was only a stony mound; what might be supposed to be a curtain with its battlements might be only a rocky crest. The mass was vague, floating, uncertain. And in the opinion of many tourists the Castle of the Carpathians existed only in the imagination of the country people. . . . . If ever a castle was a fitting refuge for the creatures of this Roumanian mythology, was it not the Castle of the Carpathians? On that isolated plateau, inaccessible except from the left of Vulkan Hill, there could be no doubt that there lived dragons and fairies and stryges, and probably a few ghosts of the family of the barons of Gortz [the former owners of the castle. I am puzzled by Verne's reference to ' stryges '. Can he mean *strigoii*?]. And so it had an evil reputation, which it deserved, as they said. No one dared to visit it. It spread around it a terrible epidemic as an unhealthy marsh gives forth its pestilential emanations. Nothing could approach it within a quarter of a mile without risking its life in this world and its salvation in the next.

Jules Verne's castle was inhabited by ghosts, Bram Stoker's by a vampire Count and three female vampires. Here we are in the realm of the Gothic horror story. It is significant that both novelists chose Transylvania, one of the remotest corners in Europe, as the setting for their tales.

Although Transylvania suffered successive invasions with the other provinces, parts were sufficiently distant, and mountainous, to remain comparatively unaffected. Maramureş, for instance, was not occupied by the Romans. There can be little doubt that Transylvania is one area in Europe which one can visit again and again and still find vestiges of past beliefs in everyday conversation in settlements only slightly distant from main highways.

Tîrgovişte, Dracula's capital, represents, in a sense, the scene of his greatest triumph, where the mighty Mohammed II, the conqueror of Constantinople, was turned back, sickened by the sight of the forest of impaled corpses and frightened by the near success of Dracula's night attack by torchlight – an extraordinarily daring feat and one quite novel in those times. Although the Sultan decided to retreat with the bulk of his army, he left behind sufficient forces to pursue Dracula across the desolate and burning Wallachian plain. It is ironical that the Sultan's forces should have included Dracula's brother, Radu the Handsome, who was later to occupy the throne of Wallachia, and four thousand Wallachian horsemen. With limited forces at his command, Dracula could never on his own defeat the Turks, but his winter campaign of 1461-2 had earned him a European reputation, and this culminated in the confrontation at Tîrgovişte the following June, a confrontation in which he was the moral if not military victor. After this Dracula's fortunes were steadily in decline: the long period of imprisonment in Hungary, his total dependence on Matthias Corvinus, his captor, and his brief occupancy of his throne in Wallachia before defeat and decapitation after death.

Tîrgovişte conveys better than Curtea de Argeş the impression of a once princely court, although only ruins remain in both centres. An exception at Tîrgovişte is the Chindia (Sunset) Tower, possibly built by Dracula himself, although some attribute the tower to his grandfather, Mircea the Old, who undoubtedly built the old palace in the fourteenth century. This tower, which was destroyed by an earthquake in 1802 and subsequently rebuilt,

offers a fine view of the remains of the royal palace. Beyond
the ruins are the fish ponds and gardens of the court, now
incorporated in a park.

As you climb the winding stairs of the tower you enter what is
virtually a Dracula museum, with maps, documents signed by
him and his seal, and other mementoes of his reigns. Any doubts
that linger that there was once a ruler of Wallachia named Vlad
the Impaler are removed here. The cellars, the best preserved
portion of the tower, contain a prison and almost certainly a
torture chamber, as at the base of the clock tower in Sighişoara.

The princely court was extended by Dracula's successors, but
it was razed time and again by invaders. For instance, between
January and May 1611 the town was conquered successively
after hard fighting by Prince Gabriel Báthory and by *voivodes*
Mihnea Şerban and Radu Şerban. Adjoining the tower are the
ruins of a small basilica, but of more interest to the visitor is the
sixteenth-century Prince's Church within the walls of the former
palace. Many of the wall paintings here are in good condition.
There is some evidence that a passage once led from the palace
to an upper section of the church where members of the royal
family sat behind curtains that shielded them from the curious
gaze of the worshippers below. A former grave just inside the
entrance to the church has been showered with silver coins which
glitter in the lamplight.

Tîrgovişte was destroyed by fire no fewer than eight times, but
no spot in Wallachia contains more memories of ancient glories.
From Mircea the Old to Prince Ghica – that is, from 1415 to
1659 – the names of more than forty *voivodes* have been connected with this capital city – proof indeed that the reigns of
many of them were very short. From the watch tower it is
possible to see the famous Monastery of the Hill where some of
these rulers are buried.

Tîrgovişte, which today has a population of 40,300, was
capital of Wallachia from the beginning of the fifteenth century
until 1660, when the seat of government was removed to
Bucharest. It might have remained a sleepy little country town
such as Curtea de Argeş were it not for the discovery of oilfields

there at the beginning of the century and by the later development of the alloy steel industry. William Forwood in his *Romanian Invitation* points out that 'the horizon of Tîrgovişte is a motley of church towers and oil derricks', a shrewd observation because it symbolizes the merging of the old with the new in Romania.

Tîrgovişte is today an important industrial centre, the largest in Romania for the production of alloy steels. It is estimated that in 1980 one million tons of alloy steels will be produced here and the town ranks second after Ploieşti in the output of oil equipment. Tîrgovişte is also a rapidly growing town and this has meant that the planners have had to decide how best to incorporate the historical and architectural features of the old capital with the flats and other buildings needed for a population which is expected to rise by 40,000 in the next twenty years.

If Dracula stood in his watch tower today he would see below him the ruins of his former court and beyond that not the Turks or a hostile army from Transylvania but a growing industrial town. Is this sad? Possibly for romantics, but no country can live only on its memories, or it will decay. The practical Romanians believe that Tîrgovişte can be both a place of memories for tourists on the Dracula circuit and also a centre for industry; this requires skill in town planning and the preservation of the historic monuments in which the town abounds.

Transylvania is the country of the fictional Dracula, and you can always travel there in imagination and people it with the vampires of Bram Stoker's tale. But, as I have tried to indicate, there is another Transylvania where stories from the past still linger, stories even stranger than the one related by Stoker, and also more authentic as examples of folk beliefs.

6 The strange world of ghosts

Many modern writers affirm that belief in vampires is held in many parts of Romania, and more particularly in Transylvania, but I did not find any of the scholars I interviewed subscribed to this idea – indeed, they were scornful of it. Vampires, I was told again and again, were a product of the fiction writer's imagination. But, I argued with myself, how could a belief be held so widely without some basis of fact behind it, and I feel the answer is that in past times bodies were sometimes staked in the grave to prevent the occupant from becoming not a vampire but a *strigoi*, or ghost.

The ghosts of Romanian folklore differ widely from those recorded by the British and American Societies for Psychical Research who classify them as mental phenomena, although, it should be stressed, neither society has a corporate view. The Romanian *strigoi* may be a living person, or the physical body of a dead one, but not, apparently, a phantom. The word *strigoi* (feminine *strigoaie*) is a word of Latin origin and in the plural is *strigoii*. A particular ghost is referred to as *strigoiul*. The Greek synonym is *bosorcoi*. The term *moroi* is sometimes used for the ghost of a dead person. There are many references in Romanian folklore to the witch or *vrăjitor* (plural *vrăjitori*, feminine *vrăjitoare*). A person described as a witch while living could become a *strigoi* after death.

According to the distinguished folklorist, Dr Katharine M. Briggs, accounts of corporeal ghosts occur in a scattered way in folk tradition. The example that would probably occur to British readers is the ballad 'The Suffolk Miracle' in which the ghost of the lover comes to fetch the girl home, and in the course of their ride she ties a red handkerchief around his head because he

complains of a headache, but when she gets to her father's door
he disappears. She then learns for the first time that he has been
dead for some weeks. The body is disinterred, and a red handkerchief is found round his head. The modern version of 'The
Suffolk Miracle' is 'The Ghostly Hitchhiker' which is current
in the United States.

Most of the corporeal ghosts are dangerous and vindictive,
particularly the Scandinavian ghosts, like the ghost of Glam in
The Saga of Grettir the Strong, and the *Barrow Wights,* according to Dr Briggs. She adds in her *Dictionary of British Folk Tales*
that the beliefs shown by these animated corpse tales 'are
extremely primitive'.

An interesting story of a corporeal ghost in the collection of the
Institute for Ethnological and Dialectological Research (formerly
the Institute of Ethnography and Folklore) in Bucharest was
related by Dr Corneliu Bărbulescu, Principal Scientific Researcher there, in the course of three long interviews he kindly
gave me.

In this tale a young man appeared at a gathering of girls and
talked until midnight. One of the girls, curious about his identity,
tied a thread to one of his boots and noticed then that he had
horses' legs – in folk belief one of the marks of a *strigoi.* After the
stranger left she followed the thread and found that it led to a
grave.

The next evening the youth reappeared and invited the girl to
go for a walk but in the course of it she managed to get rid of
him and fled to a house, where she locked the door and turned
all the pots upside down – it is a folk belief that if pots and
glasses are turned upside down ghosts are kept away (a functional
belief, as Dr Bărbulescu pointed out, because vessels open at the
top can harbour spiders and other insects). The youth started
shouting 'Pot come down and open the door', but one by one
the pots replied 'I cannot do that because I am upside down'.
Unfortunately, the girl had overlooked an oil lamp in the rafters
and this lamp obeyed the *strigoi's* summons, but as it was cracked
it broke on falling. At that moment a cock crowed to herald the
dawn and the *strigoi* disappeared.

The Institute, which was founded in 1949, contains hundreds of case reports, many of them taken down by tape recorder in the field, often from old people, and thus is a treasure house of folk beliefs which otherwise would have perished. These beliefs represented an oral tradition which had been held collectively, in its varying aspects, throughout the centuries and was free of the mentality of people in modern times which was constantly changing, Dr Bărbulescu pointed out. Oral tradition was quite different from literary tradition, and for this reason he was critical of some of the legends ascribed to Romania in Sir James Frazer's *The Golden Bough*.

Another method of warding off ghosts was to rub a person all over with garlic which had been crushed to a paste while making the sign of the cross. In Romanian folk belief garlic was regarded as a very good remedy against disease. Garlic was sometimes placed in the mouth of a dead person suspected of having been a witch. Such witches were mostly gipsy women.

According to folk belief, people who had led evil lives could become ghosts after death. You could also become a ghost if you slept out of doors on St Andrew's night. Stillborn children became ghosts. If a cat jumped over a body in a coffin the corpse would become a ghost. In some villages it is the custom to smear the doors of the stables with garlic and valerian on the night of St George to prevent witches from suckling cows. In the last century, according to Mrs Gerard, peasants kept watch over their sleeping cattle on St George's night. This same night, she said, was the best one for seeking treasure.

What harm can ghosts do? According to Dr Bărbulescu, ancient beliefs still persist in isolated places that ghosts can frighten children and also adults whose face, as a result, can become twisted; cattle can become ill, and illness spread in a village as the result of the activities of a ghost. It was also believed that a ghost could damage crops or blossom on a fruit tree by causing a sudden freeze or making hail fall. The ghostly return of a dead husband or wife could torture the feelings of the surviving partner of the marriage and harm or even kill the new husband or wife if remarriage had taken place.

I was greatly interested in Dr Bărbulescu's remarks on the folk belief that a dead person can reappear to the surviving partner of a marriage. Such a belief has some parallel in the Western world. Dr W. Dewi Rees, a Welsh general practitioner, published in the 2 October 1971 issue of the *British Medical Journal* the results of a survey of 293 of his patients who had lost their marriage partner through death. Dr Rees said that widows and widowers who sensed the presence of their former marriage partner were in no way unusual. Nearly half the patients had had some sensation of the presence of their spouse, and in many it had persisted over several years, although overall the tendency was for the sensation to become less frequent. Ten per cent of those questioned had spoken to or heard the voice of his or her partner, and a similar proportion had seen the apparition of the dead partner. Very few of the patients had spoken to their families about the matter, often because of fear or ridicule or because the experience was felt to be a private matter.

Confirmation of Dr Rees's findings is provided by Dr Colin Murray Parkes, consultant psychiatrist at St Christopher's Hospice, Sydenham, London, who interviewed twenty-one widows to assess their psychological reaction to loss. In the *British Journal of Psychiatry* for September 1975 he said that a sense of the presence of the dead husband near at hand was described by over a third of the widows at the time of the first interview carried out between four and eight weeks after the death of their partner, and three-quarters of them reported this phenomenon at some time after bereavement. Further confirmation of Dr Rees's finding is given in *Dying* by Dr John Hinton, Professor of Psychiatry at the Middlesex Hospital School, in which he says that

It is a dramatic but quite common event for the bereaved to have the experience of apparently seeing or hearing the dead person. Quite normal people, grieving over their loss, have glimpses of the person who has died. They may hear the familiar voice, perhaps saying their name, or recognize the footsteps or customary noises about the house. Usually it is soon realized that this is a trick of the senses, but the experience is often extraordinarily vivid and apparently real. People having such hallucinations may wonder if they are going mad, but it usually comforts them to know that many other sane people have similar experiences following bereavement.

I pointed out to Dr Bărbulescu that in view of the findings of the doctors quoted here it is not surprising that the bereaved partner of a marriage may believe that the dead husband or wife has returned as a *strigoi*. He commented on the belief held in Romania that a dead person returns to his home for forty days after death (a service is often held by the *popa* to mark the end of this period).

Another tradition of Romanian folklore is that when a body bleeds after death the corpse could return as a *strigoi*, although it is not a general belief that every bleeding body makes this ghostly transformation.

Ghosts took different forms in different localities, said Dr Bărbulescu. In Moldavia, for instance, there is an ancient belief in the *zmeu*, a ghostly figure quite different from the *strigoi*. It is a long flame which at night enters the room of a young girl or widow and there transforms itself into a man. Such figures did not cause the woman to become pregnant.

Twenty years ago Dr Bărbulescu was told by a farmer's wife in Moldavia that she knew a young woman who was visited by a *zmeu* but he did not interview the person concerned. Belief in the *zmeu* was not generally held in Transylvania, where the local legend, particularly in the northern part of the region, was that of the 'girl of the woods', or 'forest maiden', a beautiful figure without a back who would tempt shepherds to make love to her and as a reward lead them to the best pastures. In order to protect a boy against the forest maiden a woman would rub his body with a mixture of garlic, candle wax and the herb *rostopasca* (celandine, a member of the poppy family).

A story about the *zmeu* was told to me by Professor Dumitru Pop, Dean of the Faculty of Philology at Cluj University. He heard it from a woman of about forty in the Apuseni Mountains in mid-western Transylvania. It concerned a girl married to a dim-witted man whom she did not love. They were visited by a *zmeu* which took the form of another legendary figure the *zburător* (flyer). On many nights the sound of rattling chains announced the arrival of the flyer. As the windows were flung open the superstitious husband dived under the bedclothes and the wife disappeared with the *zburător,* only to reappear later. She became pregnant but only because she had been with a former lover who had masqueraded as the flyer (a distinction should be made between *zburător,* a folk character in European mythology and *zmeu,* the specific Romanian folk tradition).

In Marcu Beza's book *Paganism in Roumanian Folklore* the writer, who was a lecturer at King's College, London University, tells of a princess imprisoned in her room in a castle, where she is visited by 'a superhuman, legendary spirit called *zmeu,* who can assume all shapes. He is then passing by as a wind and, fluttering round the face and shoulders of the princess, he is seized by a violent love of her and swears she must be his. And the next evening he became a star and darted into the maiden's room. But there he changed into a handsome, dazzling youth. . . .'

There are other strange legendary beings in Romanian folklore. In 1951 Dr Bărbulescu taped a story by a woman of thirty-one who said that she had seen a witch (*solomonar,* not to be confused with *strigoi*) coming out of a lake riding a dragon (*balaur*). After ascending into the clouds the *solomonar* hurled hail into the garden of a man who had not shown him charity when he entered his house in human form. After this the witch disappeared on his dragon. This story, Dr Bărbulescu said, was told to him in a village in mid-western Moldavia in the area of the Ceahlău mountains.

People born with the remnants of a tail became ghosts or were known as ghosts. Dr Bărbulescu saw someone with this abnormality when he was a boy and bathing with other youths in a river. The boy with a tail was referred to as a *strigoi,* but not to his face.

I was curious about this human 'tail,' and made inquiries from a number of doctors of my acquaintance, but as none had ever seen an example of it I turned to the Royal College of Surgeons of England, which kindly supplied the information that it normally exists in a vestigial form as the coccyx which forms the lowest part of the vertebral column and is situated below the sacrum which is the fused vertebrae which form the back of the pelvis. The coccyx is normally made up of four vertebrae which are themselves fused together although the upper surface of the top one articulates with the lower surface of the sacrum. The actual number of vertebrae making up the coccyx is variable and can be more or less than four.

In tailed animals the coccyx is extended by additional bones which are free from the body, whereas in the human, under normal circumstances, it is invisible and lies at the top of the cleft of the buttocks. There have been recorded cases of minor congenital abnormality where the lower part of the coccyx lies above the normal surface of the body, although covered with skin, thus forming a tiny ' tail '.

Some of these ' tails ' are far from being tiny, judging by accounts in *Anomalies and Curiosities of Medicine* by George M. Gould and Walter L. Pyle, who report that ' Traditions of tailed men are old and widespread, and tailed races were supposed to reside in almost every country.' The authors say that Struys, a Dutch traveller in Formosa in the seventeenth century, describes a wild man caught and tied for execution who had a tail more than a foot long, which was covered with red hair like that of a cow. Oliver Wendell Holmes in the *Atlantic Monthly,* June 1890, says that he saw in London a photograph of a boy with a considerable tail. The ' Moi Boy ' was a lad of twelve, found in Cochin China, with a tail a foot long which was simply a mass of flesh. A writer in 1881 tells of a West Point student who had an elongation of the coccyx, forming a protuberance which bulged very visibly under the skin. Exercise at the riding school always gave him great distress, and the protuberance would often chafe until the skin was broken, the blood trickling into his boots.

A number of well-known scientists, including Darwin, have given accounts of ' tails '. Dr Ornstein, chief physician of the

Greek army, described a Greek of twenty-six who had a hairless, conical tail, free only at the tip, two inches long and containing three vertebrae. He also remarked that other instances had been observed in recruits. However, I have not found any reference to people with 'tails' being regarded as living 'ghosts'.

When Dr Dumitru Pop visited a village in northern Transylvania in 1949 he taped an account of a recent happening which had caused great excitement there. A woman called Floarea living alone in a lonely house on the outskirts of the village was rumoured to be a *strigoi* because she was said to have a tail. The children in the village were curious to see Floarea to establish whether she had a tail or not : her face and legs were hairy and these were other characteristics of a *strigoi*. Also, she lived near the bed of a creek along which, it was believed, ghosts could travel. There were wild cats in the neighbourhood. Could not ghosts take the shape of a cat or any other animal? The matter seemed to be put beyond doubt when one of the village women, a hoaxer, declared that she had seen Floarea's tail.

Among the villagers was a man of sixty, Florea Anii, who was superstitious and illiterate but a good narrator of stories. One evening Florea went to a sheepfold to collect milk. On his return journey he made a detour to avoid the *strigoi's* lonely home and ran into trouble. When he was crossing the creek he saw fireflies which he assumed to be ghosts and started running. The mewing of a cat reinforced his belief that ghosts were roaming that night and this added speed to his heels. He blundered into a thorn bush, cutting himself, changed direction and soon was lost. Milk slopped from his pail; in his terror he even forgot to cross himself.

One of Florea Anii's daughters, wondering what had happened to him, went at midnight to the sheepfold where he had obtained his milk and, not finding him there, started searching. Her father returned at dawn weary and scratched by thorns. The next day the old man believed that he had been chased all night by the ghost, and in his account told how he kept seeing the face of the ghost in front of him.

Dr Pop, arriving a few days later, found Florea Anii telling his story to a circle of fourteen people. 'I am an old man,' he said. 'I knew that ghosts exist, but until now God has protected me.'

Dr Pop, relating this to me, added 'Florea Anii told his story extremely well. It was one of the most beautifully told stories I have ever heard, and kept belief in ghosts alive in that village for a few more years.'

Dr Gheorghe Pavelescu, a lecturer in the Faculties of Philology and History of the University of Cluj at Sibiu who has studied folklore for over forty years, told me that according to tradition there were two ways of dealing with the ghost of a dead person.

The first was when he troubled his own family. Then it would be up to the family to act. The second was when the whole community was struck by a massive disaster, such as an epidemic. In former times the whole village would go to the cemetery and search for the *strigoi* or *moroi*. The search started with the latest burial. If the body was in a normal position the next most recent grave was opened. A body that was not in a normal position or was not decayed would be impaled by a two-pronged iron fork.

I gathered from other researchers that in some districts a wooden stake was used. The corpse could be staked in the grave through the heart or navel (the navel was regarded as the place where the child was linked with the mother), but mostly through the heart. Evidence of bodies being staked sometimes came to light when bones were collected from a grave seven years after burial, as is common in some parts of Romania, for reburial elsewhere, possibly in the vaults of a church.

Under the heading 'A contemporary Romanian vampire' Raymond T. McNally tells in *A Clutch of Vampires* how in 1969 he was passing through the village of Rodna, near the Borgo (Bîrgău) Pass, when, noticing a burial taking place in the village graveyard, he stopped to watch. 'As I talked with some of the bystanders, they told me that the deceased was a girl from the village who had died by suicide. The villagers were afraid that she would become a vampire after death. So they did what had to be done – and what I had read about for so many years.

They plunged a stake through the heart of the corpse.'

This first-hand account seemed to me to be so interesting that I referred it to Dr Bărbulescu for his opinion, asking if there was any belief in Romania that suicides should be staked in the grave. He replied that there was no such belief and the observation of Dr McNally was 'a singular incident and a probable erroneous interpretation of the things discussed with the people from Bîrgău'.

Professor Pavelescu said that the staking of a body in the grave occurred occasionally in various regions up to the time of the second world war. The last to be reported was in the Haţeg area, in south-western Transylvania, in 1937.

Haţeg is a region particularly rich in folklore traditions. In the early years of the eighteenth century a so-called *moroi* epidemic broke out in mountain villages in the Haţeg countryside and in other parts of the western mountains. The Austro-Hungarian Government sent a Dr Thaler to investigate. He reported that people were dying of a vitamin deficiency; the outbreak was confined to Romanians in the higher reaches and had not affected German communities in the lower parts of the mountains who grew peppers.

When a body was being washed after death examination might reveal the remnants of a tail. If the face still looked life-like and ruddy the mourners would put nails in the mouth and pieces of iron under the head as a reminder to the corpse what to expect if he emerged later as a *strigoi*. The grave of such a person would be the first to be opened in former times if an epidemic broke out in that neighbourhood and, if the face were still ruddy, the corpse would be staked in the coffin.

Dr Pavelescu said that, according to tradition, people who left the grave disturbed cattle by their reappearance. For this reason the widow talked to the cattle and told them that their owner had died. In former times a widow would be told to go to her husband's grave and throw soil on it so that the dead man would not return. In remote villages people still cast earth on a grave to prevent the return of the dead.

The chairs or tables on which the coffin had rested would be turned upside down to prevent the return of the dead. Even in the cities beliefs such as this were held in the early 1900s. Mirrors were covered while a corpse remained in a house. The reason for this was to prevent the dead man, if he was still there, ie. in a state of survival in some form, from seeing in the mirror that he was without a body, and the mourners from seeing their sad faces. This practice of covering or reversing mirrors was still carried out in many houses, although people who did so often did not know the folk belief that gave rise to the custom.

Mrs Gerard said in her book that 'The skull of a horse placed over the gate of the courtyard, or the bones of fallen animals buried under the doorstep, are preservatives against ghosts.' As she was in Transylvania in the 1880s I wrote to Dr Bărbulescu asking if this tradition was still observed. He replied that although there was such a tradition in some regions in the past, it was not attested today and could be discovered only in fairy tales.

Dr Pavelescu, answering in a letter some points about ghosts I had raised with him in Sibiu, said that in country areas in the past people believed that

the quality of *strigoi* was given by Nature itself as an implacable destiny. According to this belief, the midwife can tell when some-body is born *strigoi* because the baby has a caul or a short tail. The midwife then can fate the newborn child and channel his *strigoi* quality to a certain direction, eg to take the milk from cows, the growth from wheat, the productivity from bees. Other *strigoi* can take [affect] the efficiency of the distaff, the hoe, the axe, the broom.

Dr Pavelescu said that during the performance of their witch-craft the *strigoii* can turn into various animals or insects: cats, dogs, wolves, horses, spiders, 'even waggon-wheels or flickers that can be seen flying at night' (an example is that of the fireflies seen by the old man and mistaken for ghosts).

According to ancient belief, the dead *strigoi* may turn into a cat, goat, horse or flies, said Dr Pavelescu, adding that 'some people think that the *strigoii* are invisible and that they are traceable only through sonorous effects: hammering, squeaking, whizzing, etc.'

Apart from stabbing the body of a person suspected of being a *strigoi* through the heart with a sharp-pointed object, another way of making the corpse harmless was by fastening the legs with rope.

The notorious Count Dracula frequently appears as a bat in Bram Stoker's novel, so that naturally I wondered if any of these transformations in Romanian folk beliefs included that of the living or dead into a bat. When I referred this point to Dr Bǎrbulescu he answered that there was no such belief, 'not even in the fairy tales'. So much for Count Dracula and bats.

When I was in Transylvania Dr Pavelescu told me that although belief in witches who could cast spells of the more powerful sort had disappeared, belief in women who could cure diseases still remained. Witches used two methods for healing : self suggestion and remedies made from plants

Witches were tolerated but they were feared. In former times people taking cows to the fields would avoid a witch's house, and if the witch came out men looking after the cattle would cover their testicles with their hands to protect themselves against the effects of the evil eye. Dr Pavelescu was told by his grandfather that if you met a man who was known as a witch or *strigoi* you took your testicles in your hand in self-protection. Renée Haynes says in *The Seeing Eye, the Seeing I* that Aldous Huxley once described an incident he had witnessed in Italy, when a regiment was reviewed by a general popularly supposed to have the evil eye. The men marched smartly past him, each saluting with his right hand and protecting his genitals with his left, extending in the traditional ' horns of the devil' sign.

I have already commented on the number of horses I have seen in Transylvania with their harnesses decorated with red tassels and the drivers of the carts with red cord or cloth tied to the whip. Although this is done now mostly for decoration, it should not be forgotten that red was formerly worn as protection against the evil eye. Dr Bǎrbulescu confirmed that red rosettes were once placed on oxen as protection against the evil eye, and there was a time when children on a farm wore red for the same purpose. Other remedies against the evil eye will be mentioned in my accounts of visits to villages in the Transylvanian country-side.

Many of the experiences related by villagers concern witches. This suggests to me that among old people at least there is still a belief in witches in Romania, a belief shared with the Western world.

In the large volume dealing with legends in *A Dictionary of British Folk Tales* Dr Briggs says that

There is no doubt that witchcraft beliefs are still alive in this country, though a great deal of the interest taken in witchcraft depends upon scepticism; it is the pleasure taken in quaint, obsolete, horrific stories which would be no pleasure at all if they were believed in. . . . The real country belief in witchcraft, with its ill-will, forespelling and sympathetic magic, has left plenty of traces all over the country, and the actual belief itself is still lurking among unsophisticated people, though no longer so explicit as it once was. This is the soil out of which the theological, intellec-tualised beliefs arose, which nourished them and made the witch persecutions possible. The more complicated and thoughtful features of the belief have faded in England and left only the basic assumptions on which they were founded. In Scotland, where the beliefs were more theological and nearer to those held on the Continent, and where the persecutions were more cruel, we find tales of the witches' Sabbat and more instances than in England of the diabolic compact. Tales of imps, familiars and shape-shifting are to be found everywhere. Everywhere dairy produce is tampered with, livestock are injured and human beings bewitched and visited with sickness or death. Everywhere witches are nasty people to annoy, and they are often retaliated on with unnecessary brutality.

Tales of shape-shifting and witches who interfere with dairy produce are frequently found in Romania.

Although Romanian folklorists deplore what they describe as 'sensational' stories about vampires based mainly on the *Dracula* cult as presented by Bram Stoker, there can be little doubt about interest – and belief – in vampires in the West. There was, for instance, the bizarre case in Stoke-on-Trent early in 1973 when a Pole who was afraid of vampires died from swallowing garlic which he had placed in his mouth for protection against them.

As added precautions he had the room strewn with salt in a ritual fashion, had a bag of salt between his legs resting on his testicles (salt was believed by him to be a vampire repellent), and had garlic round the room.

In 1969 and 1970 'vampire hunting' took place in Highgate Cemetery, north London, ending in a service of exorcism. The story started in 1967 when two schoolgirls, walking past the cemetery, saw that 'the graves were opening up, and the people were rising'. There were later reports of figures being seen in the cemetery, but there was probably a physical reason for this. Intruders could have been lurking in the cemetery, or mist figures could have been mistaken for those of humans. Whatever the explanation, the interest generated by the happenings at Highgate shows a continuing public interest in the undead, fed by a succession of Dracula films.

There can be little doubt that people suspected of being the 'undead' because of their appearance when the grave was opened were often the victims of premature burial. Gabriel Ronay says in *The Dracula Myth* that

A careful and unbiased examination of all recorded eighteenth-century vampire investigations would reveal a marked lack of reliable first-hand evidence concerning actual attacks by undead creatures. The intact bodies disinterred on suspicion of vampirism were not, in my view, in some sort of mystical vampire condition, but belonged, more likely than not, to unfortunate people who had been buried alive. Reports of people declared to be dead who revive in the morgue are quite common even in our medically advanced times, and it is quite understandable that gravely-ill patients and people subject to epileptic and other fits were buried alive in remote villages in eighteenth-century Eastern Europe.

If they were lucky they died soon, either because of their illness or as a result of asphyxiation due to the premature internment. Those in a kind of suspended animation on the border of life and death (catalepsy) could have stayed intact for a considerable time without particularly damaging effect on their bodies. On regaining consciousness, however, perhaps several days or even weeks after burial, they would naturally try to claw their way out of their tomb, and this would explain the fresh blood on their faces and their hands. The mass of evidence adduced by the vampire tribunals charged with opening the graves of suspected vampires confirms no more than this. And the alleged undead vampires, freshly dug up from their graves, who according to the vampire tribunal reports, jerked and cried out under the executioner's stake, were the sorry victims of burial alive who came to in the moment of their execution. . . .

Mr Ronay uses the term 'vampire' here, but this would be disputed by the scholars I quote who prefer the term 'ghost' for this figure of ancient folk belief. Apparently there has never been a tradition of blood sucking in Romanian folklore.

Dr Bărbulescu told me that, according to folk tradition, one way of preventing a corpse from becoming a *strigoi* was to reverse the position of the body in the grave.

A burial custom mentioned by Marcu Beza is that of preparing food and drink for the last journey of the departed. 'For three consecutive nights after burial, the peasants are careful to put out for the deceased, on the very spot in the house where the body was laid, a vessel of wine or water and a cake. The fact points to the folk belief in the preservation of the soul's individuality and, to a certain extent, to its continued earthly needs.'

This belief in food and drink being necessary for the dead on their last journey is, of course, common to many countries.

Many Romanian folk traditions concern sheep. Dr Dumitru Pop said that one of the most popular legends, found among the Greeks, Bulgarians, Serbs, Poles and Romanians, is that of the looted sheepfold. One version of the legend tells of a shepherd who was surprised by thieves. They killed his dogs, tied his hands, and were about to leave with the sheep when he asked them to untie one hand so that he could play his flute. The thieves agreed to this apparently harmless request, but the tune which the shepherd played was heard by people in the village nearby who recognized it as a call for help and came to the rescue.

Romania has an unwritten law that a woman does not herd sheep. If she did mishaps would follow: the sheep might rush about wildly or the milk be lost or spoiled. In former times it was believed, and in some parts is still believed, that a woman experiencing her monthly period should not go near sheep because of the effect this would have on them, although in the Maramureş version of the looted sheepfold the shepherd is a woman.

As no documents have come down from the Dacians, former rulers of the country, we did not know if this prohibition of women associating with sheep belonged to them, but as Maramureş was never under Roman rule it is possible that it was not affected by the practices in regions which were under the Romans and therefore this belief – that the association of women with sheep brought tragedy – could have always been there. If this were so, the attack by the robbers was probably a punishment for a woman's action in looking after sheep.

Within the past two years Dr Pop took a party of students to a valley fifty miles north-west of Cluj where an interesting local custom was observed. While the sheep were in winter quarters the women were allowed to behave in as unruly manner as they wished, but when the sheep were released to go to mountain pastures all such behaviour had to stop.

How, then, are we to regard the strange world of ghosts revealed here? The answer, I feel, will be found in the particular field to which the reader gives his attention. In the Western world the study of apparitions is regarded as a scientific discipline in parapsychology, so that H. H. Price, Wykeham Professor of Logic at Oxford from 1935 to 1959, in his preface to *Apparitions* by G. N. M. Tyrrell, can say that

The tea-party question, 'Do you believe in ghosts?' is one of the most ambiguous which can be asked. But if we take it to mean, 'Do you believe that people sometimes experience apparitions?' the answer is that they certainly do. No one who examines the evidence can come to any other conclusion. Instead of disputing the facts, we must try to explain them. But whatever explanation we offer, we soon find ourselves in very deep waters indeed.

Professor Price goes on to say that the pre-scientific theory of apparitions (if anything so vague could be called a theory) was that an apparition was a *physical* entity, physically present in the room or other place where the percipient was. However, there were objections to this theory, such as that 'ghosts' did not leave any physical traces behind them, like footprints. In fact, says Professor Price, the difficulties in the way of this physical theory of apparitions are so great that we cannot be surprised if scientifically educated people refuse to 'believe in ghosts' at all, and adds that 'If a physical theory of apparitions is so unpromising, it is natural to try a psychological one instead.'

In Romania there is no body equivalent to The Society for Psychical Research, so that the folklorists, who are fulfilling a most important task in recording and classifying folk beliefs before they disappear, seek the answers in their own field of study, where they display a healthy scepticism, as do indeed all serious writers on ghosts in the West.

None of the scholars I interviewed in Romania professed a belief in ghosts. Indeed, as Dr Bărbulescu told me, 'In Romania we do not believe in *strigoii*. All these ghosts and demon-like figures are the products of oral reminiscences and it cannot be taken for granted that they exist or existed, but are inherited from tales of old people from generation to generation.'

Actually, he said, ghosts were 'metaphors' which after much repetition had become personified and were mainly the representations or imaginings of people who could not otherwise explain certain phenomena. The description and name of a particular phenomenon varied from region to region, so that there was a difference here between classical and folk mythology: in classical mythology the figure took the same form everywhere, but in folk mythology the narrator decided the form a figure should take.

Folk tales, said Dr Bărbulescu, were a psychological necessity for rural people, taking the place of works of fiction and other books. This phrase 'psychological necessity' reminded me of an earlier interview I had with Dr Mihai Pop when he was Director of the Institute of Ethnography and Folklore, a position from which he has just retired. Dr Pop had visited the United States and explained that the popularity of occultism there was 'a psychological necessity in a more industrialised society'.

So, it seems to me, ghost stories from remote villages in Transylvania and bizarre cults, such as that of Satanism in California, result from a need to believe in the miraculous and are attempts to explain the unexplainable.

7 Werewolves and other transformations

The voice on the tape was old and crackling, but it told a strange story with conviction. Toma Neghină was eighty-three when he was interviewed by Dr Bărbulescu at Boița, near Sibiu, eight years ago. He once knew, he said, a man (now dead) who turned himself at night into a wolf, joined a pack and led them to stables to attack the animals there.

Stories of werewolves (*pricolici*) are occasionally found in remote areas of Romania, where wolves still roam, although in greatly reduced numbers compared with previous years, owing to the activities of hunters. The belief in shape-shifting, in which a man can turn himself into a wolf or some other animal, has certain features in common with belief in witches and ghosts, at least in Romania. For instance, there is a folk belief that ghosts can turn people into animals and put them to work.

Wolves feature prominently in Bram Stoker's *Dracula,* as well they might, for they were a real danger to travellers in Transylvania in the last century. When Charles Boner was there in 1863 his gipsy guide pointed to a spot where his mother, while getting wood, had been eaten by three wolves.

Some of these folk tales take bizarre forms. In northern Moldavia at the end of the last century a woman related how her grandmother would leave the house at night and turn herself into a horse. When her husband asked her where she had been she said that she had gone out to fulfil her work as a *strigoi.*

In 1975 Dr Bărbulescu was taping folk tales in Bihor country, near the border with Hungary and a region rich in folklore, where he was told by a woman of seventy-three that when she was very young two women saw another woman take off her clothes and go into the forest as a she-wolf. They did not take the clothes because if they did the 'she wolf' would not be able to resume human shape.

A similar story has been told in northern Moldavia, said Dr Bărbulescu, but in this version the woman is seen to go off as a horse (it will be remembered from the previous chapter that one of the indications of a *strigoi* is that he may have the legs of a horse).

In Bihor Dr Bărbulescu was told by a man of seventy-four that when he was young he travelled with a party of men who included one who begged the others to tie him to the wheel of the cart so that he would not go off to join the wolves when they were heard howling in the distance.

This man probably suffered from lycanthropy, a psychiatric complaint known from early times. It is defined in the *Oxford English Dictionary as* 'Madness in which the patient imagines himself and acts like some beast.' Although wolves have long been extinct in Great Britain cases of lycanthropy still occur. *The Guardian* of 29 April 1975 contains an account of the inquest on a youth of seventeen who was convinced that he was turning into a werewolf. He thought his hands and face were changing colour, and he began growling. The youth was found stabbed to death in the village of Eccleshall, near Stafford. His flick-knife was found partly open near him in a pool of blood. A verdict of suicide was returned.

When Dr Pavelescu was in the Apuseni Mountains in 1939 he overheard someone talking about a woman who, when travelling, was attacked by a wolf which bit off a piece of her skirt. When she returned home she met her husband who had a bit of her skirt in his mouth. She then realized that she was married to a werewolf.

This is a variation of a story common throughout Transylvania. The most usual version is that of the newly married couple who went haymaking. In the absence of the husband the young wife is attacked by a large dog or wolf. She shouts for her husband to come to her aid while she fights off the animal's attack. After the disappearance of the animal her husband emerges from the forest. While she tells him what has happened to her he notices that a piece of cloth in his teeth is the exact match of a portion torn from her dress.

We will come across this story again, but an interesting variation of it is related by Emily Gerard in *The Land Beyond the Forest*. She says that sometimes it is a dog instead of a wolf whose form a man has taken, or been compelled to take, as penance for his sins. In one village a story is told – and believed – of such a man, who driving home one Sunday with his wife, suddenly felt that the time for his transformation had come. He therefore gave over the reins to her, and stepped aside into the bushes, where, murmuring the mystic formula, he turned three somersaults over a ditch. Soon after the woman, waiting vainly for her husband, was attacked by a furious dog, which rushed barking out of the bushes and succeeded in biting her severely as well as tearing her dress. When, an hour or two later, the woman reached home after giving up her husband as lost, she was surprised to see him coming smiling to meet her; but when between his teeth she caught sight of the shreds of her dress bitten out by the dog, the horror of this discovery caused her to faint away.

Another man used to assert gravely that for several years he had gone about in the form of a wolf, leading on a troop of these animals, till a hunter, in striking off his head, restored him to his natural shape.

This superstition, says Mrs Gerard, once proved nearly fatal to a harmless botanist, who, while collecting plants on a hillside many years ago, was observed by some peasants, and, in consequence of his crouching attitude, mistaken for a wolf. Before they had time to reach him, however, he had risen to his feet and disclosed himself in the form of a man; but this in the mind of the Romanians, who now regarded him as an aggravated case of wolf, was but additional motive for attacking him. They were quite sure that he must be a werewolf, for only such could change his shape in this unaccountable manner, 'and in another minute they were all in full cry after the wretched victim of science, who might have fared badly indeed had he not succeeded in gaining a carriage on the highroad before his pursuers came up.'

Mrs Gerard once asked an old Saxon woman whether she had ever come across a werewolf herself. 'Bless you!' she said, 'when I was young (and we remember here that this interview took place over ninety years ago) there was no village without two or three of them at least, but now there seem to be fewer.'

The Celts who settled in north and north-western Transylvania in 300 BC believed in werewolves, but such beliefs were common in ancient times. Indeed, as Dr Mihai Pop pointed out to me, the werewolf is a mythological representation common to England, France (where it is known as the *loup garou*) and Germany. As the wolf is extinct over large tracts of Europe and North America stories about werewolves tend to die out, so that it was a matter of great interest to me to discover that such stories are still coming to light in Romania.

Mrs Gerard, writing in the 1880s, said

We do not require to go far for the explanation of the extraordinary tenacity of the werewolf legend in a country like Transylvania, where real wolves still abound. Every winter here brings fresh proof of the boldness and cunning of these terrible animals, whose attacks on flocks and farms are often conducted with a skill which would do honour to a human intellect. Sometimes a whole village is kept in trepidation for weeks together by some particularly audacious leader of a [pack] of wolves, to whom the peasants not unnaturally attribute a more than animal nature; and it is safe to prophesy that as long as the flesh-and-blood wolf continues to haunt the Transylvanian forests, so long will his spectre brother survive in the minds of the people.

Usually, a person is deemed to take the form of the most dangerous beast of prey of the region: the wolf or bear in Europe and Northern Asia; the hyena or leopard in Africa, and the tiger in India, China, Japan and elsewhere in Asia, but the wolf seems to have a special place in folk beliefs of various kinds. For instance, at the exhibition of Indian art from the north-west coast of America at the Museum of Mankind, London, in 1976 it was pointed out that among the Nootka and Maksh of the southern north-west coast the wolf played an important part in the ceremonies surrounding the initiation of young novices into the associations maintaining the ritual and life of the tribes.

In the wolf ritual a dramatization of a legend takes place in which the novices are seized by wolf dancers imbued with certain characteristics of the wolf and then captured back for the tribe by older men. It was only after this ceremony, the *Klukwalle,* that young men could participate in the mainstream of tribal life.

It is interesting that stories of men changing into wolves or big dogs are also coming to light in North America. One, collected in 1955 from Pierre Pilote, aged sixty-one, in Quebec Province by M. Luc Lacourcière, Director of Les Archives de Folklore, Laval University, Quebec, is included in *Folktales Told Around the World.* This book is edited by Richard M. Dorson, distinguished Professor of History and Folklore at Indiana University and Director of the Folklore Institute there, who tells me that the archives at Laval University undoubtedly have the largest number of werewolf and big dog beliefs of any country in North America. In Canada they are known as *roup-garou* tales, differing slightly in description from the *loup-garou* stories of France.

Pierre Pilote's story is about a farmer who hires a 'big young man' about twenty to cut his hay and notices that the hired hand never ate breakfast in the morning. One moonlit night the farmer hides in the barn.

Around eleven o'clock what does the farmer see entering the courtyard? A big dog with a big leg of beef in his mouth! The dog goes under the wagon in the barn and then the man can hear bones crunching. He ate the whole thing. Then when he had finished eating his beef, the dog came out into the courtyard, and licked his paws all over. All of a sudden he turns into the young man, the hired hand!

The young man is dismissed the following morning, but not before telling the farmer 'You were lucky that I didn't see you. You would have ended up like the leg of beef. I would have eaten you too!'

The narrative ends with the remark, 'They used to say in those days that if a man didn't take the sacrament at Easter for seven years he would be changed into an animal.'

An account of a were-crocodile by a Stone Age man in Malaysia is given by Gordon Wellesley in *Sex and the Occult*. This Sakai aborigine told the writer that he had once been seized by a crocodile while fishing, but his cries were heard and his two sons raced to the rescue,

one to begin the customary tug-of-war with the scaly brute while the other hacked at it with a parang. Eventually the jaws loosened and his sons and others of the little tribe continued the good work until the attacker was dismembered and the remnants thrown back into the bloodied water to be devoured completely by its carrion-loving fellows. This, I was to understand, had great importance since otherwise the creature would have become a man again.

The aborigine explained that his assailant was clearly recognizable by certain signs as a *halak* (shaman) who had been his enemy. This particular *halak* was never seen again. 'It was known that he had left his village on the day in question, paddling down-stream towards the Sakai camp. He never returned and after many days his *prahu* was found hidden in the undergrowth beside the river bank, undamaged. In it was a bag containing the materials for spells, including a pot of ointment used for transformation into animal form.'

Mr Wellesley asked the country's Commissioner for Wild Life, Colonel Hubback, what credence, if any, should be attached to this tale of the were-crocodile. 'His answer, rich fruit of a life-time in the jungle, was simple: "I *dis*believe in nothing!"'

So it will be seen that Transylvania is not the only country that contains strange beliefs, although few have so rich and varied a folklore. From time to time I am asked to write articles for newspapers or magazines on vampires and my answer always is that there is little real evidence for a belief that the dead leave the grave to drink the blood of the living. On the other hand, there has been wide belief since the earliest times that men and women can, under certain conditions, take the shape of animals, but I would need a lot of convincing that such a transformation actually takes place. In other words, there is a real folk belief in werewolves and other were-animals but not, outside fiction, in vampires, although, as has been indicated earlier, such tales of the undead seem to fill a psychological need.

8 Sibiu and tales from the villages

Sibiu is an old town connected with Dracula in which the past casts a long shadow. It was to become his chief refuge in Transylvania after release from the long period of captivity in Hungary, but it had incurred his wrath during his second and principal reign when he was in dispute with the Saxons over political and trade issues and because he suspected them of harbouring claimants to his throne. Ladislas Posthumus was then on the throne of Hungary, with the support of the Saxons, but Matthias Corvinus was a contender and Dracula favoured his cause. For this reason Ladislas began to champion anti-Dracula candidates, including Vlad the Monk, his half brother, who were currying favour with the Saxons in Transylvania.

We see Dracula at his most ruthless when he made a lightning raid into the Sibiu district in 1457, burning castles and villages and the suburbs of the town. Men, women and children perished in the flames. How different it was in 1475 when Dracula asked permission from the citizens of Sibiu for the construction of a house for himself and his family. The King of Hungary sent two hundred florins to Dracula, who was then living in the neighbouring village of Balcaciu, to help him with the expenses of this house. Dracula, who, according to tradition, was fond of referring to himself as 'a great ruler', was now a supplicant, as was his father, Vlad Dracul, when he asked the municipality of Sighişoara for a house. Time has its vengeance on the proud.

Perhaps this judgement is, in certain respects, unfair. As Boner points out,

The jealousy with which the Saxons guarded their rights of citizenship against encroachment is a marked feature in their history. No Hungarian was allowed to possess land or a dwelling on Saxon ground. Every attempt to do so was resisted pertinaciously and at once. Even if by will, house or land had been left to a Hungarian, it was sold, and the money handed over to him; but on Saxon soil he was allowed to have no footing. In such wise did this handful of strangers exclude every element which might possibly interfere with their peculiar political life. They feared, and justly, that a beginning once made, there would soon be a preponderance in their administration of aims and interests different from their own; and they determined that, under no pretext whatever, should such beginning ever take place. How unflinching their opposition is shown by the continued defeat of the Hungarian nobility in all their attempts to obtain citizenship among them. And bold indeed must have been the front they showed – these German immigrants, tillers of the soil, traders and workers at the loom and various handicrafts – to have opposed successfully sovereign and minister, and the highest authorities of the Church; a powerful nobility, too, proud of its position, and unaccustomed to give way to a plebian will. Yet this, more than once, these men did; they fought their own battle and won it; and, moreover, unaided and alone.

So it was a real privilege that Dracula, even with the support of the great Matthias Corvinus, should have been allowed to build a house in this Saxon stronghold. He was no Hungarian, it is true, but he represented Hungarian influence. The city authorities must have given long and careful consideration to his application to build a home there. What probably influenced their decision to grant it was the thought that he had raided the town and district eighteen years previously and, once back on the throne of Wallachia, might do so again on the grounds that the civic authorities had refused to give hospitality to a 'great ruler', although their sovereign had requested it.

The location of Dracula's home is not known today, but it could be any of the old houses in the squares in the medieval parts of the town, including the one in which the Evangelical Church stands. It was after attending a service in this church, then a Roman Catholic Cathedral, that Mihnea the Bad, the Impaler's eldest surviving son, who ruled Wallachia from April 1508 to October 1509, was stabbed to death on 12 March 1510

E

by one of his political opponents. His grave is in the crypt. Mihnea seems to have had all his father's bad qualities and none of his considerable virtues.

Sibiu, which now has a population of 150,000 people and is in many respects the cultural capital of Transylvania, was old in Dracula's time, remote as that now seems. Stone age remains have been found in the town; a Daco-Roman village grew up round the castrum of Cedonia there, built by the Romans to watch over the road which led from the Olt Valley into the heart of Transylvania, and the Saxons came in the twelfth century, adding their numbers to the original Romanian population which was already organized in its own political forms. The town was built between 1141 and 1161. The first mention of Sibiu is as Cibinium in twelfth-century documents, a name borrowed from the Cibin river which flows from the Cibin Mountains.

The Saxons, who called the town Hermannstadt, built a small citadel on the river terrace above the Cibin, but it was destroyed by the Tartars in 1241. The Tartars, however, never represented the recurring danger as invaders that the Turks did. Towards the end of the fourteenth century the inhabitants of Sibiu built strong brick walls around the upper town which was called 'the red town' by the Turks from the colour of its brick walls. The fortifications successfully withstood the Turkish attacks of 1432, 1438 and 1442, and were continuously expended so that eventually there were three rings of walls and forty defence towers. This successful defiance of the Turks encouraged other Transylvanian towns to surround themselves with walls. The Turkish leader, when besieging Sibiu with 70,000 men in 1438, was killed by an arrow fired from one of the towers. Possibly this is the origin of the legend of the Pasha and his elephant at Sighişoara.

Parts of Sibiu still convey, to a remarkable degree, an impression of a German town of former days. Boner, who was there in 1863, said that 'On your very entrance to the town, as you come from the west, you are reminded of some old place or other seen in Germany, and dating from the Middle Ages. The street is steep and narrow, and winds past ancient walls; and as the

coach lumbers on to the Post Office, you might, for aught you
see to the contrary, be entering Ausburg, or Nürnberg, or Ulm.'

When Dr Starkie was in Sibiu in 1929 the towns was still

sad and mysterious . . . it did not seem to be in Transylvania,
for it had no Romanian or Hungarian characteristics. Everywhere
I went I could see old watchtowers, ramparts, houses with heavy
grated windows that recalled sieges of long ago. Its Saxon origin
had given the town a certain air of austere gravity, but in addition
there was an air of mystery about these crooked streets with their
countless tunnels connecting one another. It is said that these
tunnels are relics of the old days, when the Turks were the terror
of the country.

Dr Starkie also found that 'at night the streets are silent and
the people who walk about do not sing or talk loudly.' Mrs
Gerard considered the town to be depressingly dull in winter
when she was there over ninety years ago.

What is usually understood by the word amusement did not here
exist. There is a theatre, it is true, but this is available in summer
only; for as the crazy old tower which has been turned into a temple
of the muses cannot be heated, it remains closed till the return
of spring brings with the swallows some theatrical company of
third or fourth class to delight the population during a space of
some weeks. Now and then a shabby menagerie or still shabbier
circus finds its way to the place; and such minor attractions as an
educated seal, a fat lady, or a family of intelligent fleas offer themselves for the delectation of a distinguished public. I have known
persons who paid as many as six visits to the seal and eight to the
fat lady during this period of vital stagnation. Is not this bare
statement wellnigh pathetic in its dreary suggestiveness? What
stronger proof can there be of the mournful state of an intellect
reduced to seek comfort from seals or fat women?

There are better attractions than seals and fat women in Sibiu
today. The State Theatre gives performances in Romanian and
German; there is the State Philharmonic Orchestra, folk music
bands, a puppet theatre, and, as in most centres, a House of
Culture. Romanians, I have found on my many visits, have a
fondness for old musical comedies. When you are sitting alone in

a restaurant or with your interpreter the strains of the 'Indian Love Call' from *Rose Marie* or 'You are my Heart's Delight' from *The Land of Smiles* can send you wandering down memory lane. Sibiu is rapidly getting up to date. The local jazz club is the most important and active in Romania, with not only hundreds of active members but also three jazz bands of different styles, and since 1974 the National Jazz Festival has been held in the town.

Whenever I am in Sibiu I get the impression that I am being followed by eyes in the attics of tall houses. These are small windows set in the steep roof in such a way that the shaped eaves have the appearance of lids. The attics are used for the storage of food.

Sibiu has more than doubled in population since Dr Starkie was there and is much more Romanian in appearance than before, but the contrast between the modern and medieval parts of the town is still great. The building of factories has been accompanied by the construction of flats for the increasing population. Sibiu was an important handicraft ware centre in the fourteenth century. It was in this century that Sibiu obtained the right to hold fairs and became a free city. Much of its trade was with Wallachia. The main industries now are the manufacture of machines, agricultural implements, precision tools, petrochemical plants and products and furniture.

Sibiu is famous for the Brukenthal Museum created by Samuel Brukenthal, Governor of Transylvania between 1777 and 1787, in his Austrian baroque palace with his own collection of paintings, art objects, engravings and books. Some of the paintings are masterpieces of great value. The library of the museum has 220,000 volumes and many documents relating to the history of Transylvania. The museum even has its own ghost story. As related by Mrs Gerard, an old soldier coming home from the wars is met by three old men in turn to whom he gives his last three coins. The third man then said 'See, I am one and the same as the two old men who begged from you before, and am none other than Christ the Lord. As, therefore, you have been charitable, and have given of the little you had, so will I reward you by granting any boon you choose to ask.' The soldier begged for a sack which should have the virtue that, whenever he spoke the words, 'Pack yourself in the sack,' man or beast should equally be obliged to creep inside it. With this magic sack on his back the soldier tramped on till he reached Sibiu. Here he found all the population talking of a ghost in the Bruckenthal palace which had lately been disturbing the place, and whoever attempted to pass the night in the rooms of the palace was found a corpse the next day. The soldier was given permission by Baron Bruckenthal to spend the night in the palace although he was warned of the dangers. The soldier managed to 'bag' the ghost, which in the course of seeking release from the sack revealed that in the walls there were concealed many barrels containing treasures and it was his mission to watch over them. Next morning the inhabitants were greatly astonished to find the soldier still alive. Under his direction the walls were broken open and within many little barrels were discovered, all containing heavy gold, of which the brave soldier received a handsome portion, sufficient to enable him to live in comfort to the end of his days.

This pleasant but most unlikely story belongs to legend, as does the tale of the Pasha and his elephant, so that it was with the hope of getting accounts of experiences more closely allied to genuine folk beliefs that I met Dr Pavelescu, who has been collecting such accounts for the greater part of his life. He took me to Sibiel, a village of between 700 and 800 people, fifteen miles north-west of Sibiu. It was a clear day in early Spring and we had a good view of the snow-covered Cibin Mountains. The last three-quarters of a mile was over a rough track past fields in which two youths in long sheepskin coats watched their flocks.

As in so many Romanian villages, the young people had gone to the town for work. A service marking the anniversary of a death forty days earlier had just finished and, as was the usual custom, we were offered țuică (plum brandy), all drinking from the same glass, and bread with salt. The middle-aged and elderly women wore black, some with white aprons. The old church here has a museum containing icons painted on glass and among the books a copy of the first Bible printed in Romania in 1688 – the Cyrillic alphabet was used for this.

Dr Pavelescu was obviously at home in the village. He led me through a typical Transylvanian courtyard to where Maria Dăncilă, aged ninety-four, sat in her crowded little room. Religious pictures, small mats, pots and pans and other objects jostled for space on the wall. Maria was born in this village, but fifty years ago worked in Chicago in a factory which made pottery and also in one which made glue, so that it cannot be said that her beliefs are the result of lack of contact with the outside world.

Maria said that she believed firmly in witches, both male and female, known locally as ghosts *(strigoi* or *strigoaie)*, who could take milk from a cow. When such witches were born they had a form of tail and they also had a dark-coloured spot on the head with hair on it, but this spot could be washed away at birth. All who saw a child with such physical characteristics knew that it was a witch. Even if these indications of a witch were not noticed at birth they were observed when the baby was bathed. No one would take action against such a person because it was God's will. Witches bathed in a river or lake at midnight, always alone so as to avoid being seen. Witches not only took milk from cows and sheep but affected them so that they behaved in a disturbed manner ('wild way' was the phrase used). Witches also took the cream away from the milk while it was still in the cow and took away the centre of the grain so that it could not be sown again.

'People cannot fight against witchcraft – they are powerless – but a cow's milk does return,' the old woman declared.

People on whom the gaze of a witch fell had as a result a terrible headache which could be removed by placing nine charred pieces of wood, still hot, in a glass of water, three at a time, at intervals during which magic words were spoken or the Lord's Prayer recited. If the pieces of wood fell to the bottom the headache disappeared, but the water was sipped just the same and then thrown away so that the witchcraft went with the water.

Maria said she had heard of a witch who put powder in the form of the sign of the cross on the road so that cows let out of their winter quarters for the first time in early spring lost their milk. Maria Dăncilă also believed in werewolves. They were born, she said, of the union of a brother and sister. If some animal bit a werewolf, drawing blood, it then resumed the form of a human being.

The references to the use of the charred pieces of wood in water reminded me of a passage in that striking novel of Transylvanian life, *Easter Sun* by Peter Neagoe, which was recommended to me by a Romanian scholar. The principal character, Ileana, is a girl suspected of having the evil eye. She approaches a mother suckling her baby who

was sorry that she did not cover the baby's face when Ileana came. Turning her head to one side, she spat out three times, whispering the invocation against the evil eye. Several times, pretending to caress the baby, she covered his face with her hand, but she feared that it was not enough. As soon as Ileana left, the woman ran home to 'quench embers in water', that being the remedy against the evil eye in case her abracadabra, pronounced while the girl was looking at the infant, proved ineffective. Her heart sank at the frightful augury of the embers, for as she dropped them into the water, chanting, all three dropped heavily to the bottom. But she continued the soothsaying, dipping her finger in the water and tracing crosses on the baby's forehead and in his palms. Her hand trembled as she dropped some of the water into the baby's mouth. The little fellow screwed up his face and slobbered it out, but the mother wiped it back into his mouth until she was certain that he swallowed a few drops.

The novelist gives a 'a sure cure' for jaundice the folk belief in crushed embers drunk in gold-coloured wine.

Our next call in Sibiel was at the cottage of grey-haired Dumitru Banciu, born in 1895, and his wife Maria, who was seventy-one. Both were born in the village. The husband was a shepherd from the age of eleven until the first world war. In 1907 he had his own experience of witchcraft when he was tending sheep at Bărăgan in the plains of Southern Romania.

One night, when the full moon made the scene 'almost as bright as day', a wolf came to his flock. He was only ten to fifteen yards away and saw that the wolf could not open its mouth to bite the sheep. When the dogs attacked the wolf it ran away. Before this happened he had heard in the locality that witches had the power to shut the mouths of wolves so that they would not bite sheep. It was also a tradition that if you tied a pair of scissors on the Day of St Peter and St Paul and kept them tied for two to three days you were thereby tying the mouth of the wolf. '*Filipii*' was the name given to this practice.

The former shepherd said that about ten years ago he had heard in the mountains about people who, by looking at sheep, not only took away their ability to give milk but even to eat properly. Another way to keep wolves away from sheep was for a naked man to march around the flock at midnight uttering incantations, he stated.

Maria Banciu told of a neighbour, a woman of Russian descent, who had lost the milk of her cow because a woman had left two empty pails in her courtyard (even today it is believed that no one should enter a courtyard with empty vessels if the owner of the house has a cow in milk). In order to break the spell the cow's owner went to another village to see a witch who advised her to take a new empty ceramic vessel which should not be covered and boil in it the urine of the cow. While this was being done the door of the courtyard should be kept locked. The person who cast the spell that took away the cow's milk would have a boiling feeling and come to the house to ask for something to take the pain away. Sure enough, an old woman came knocking on the door and asked for vegetables, which were given. When she reported this to the witch the woman was told to give maize to the old woman's cow and by this means milk would be restored to her cow. Milk did return, but not to the same extent as before.

Late that afternoon we went to the attractive village of Rǎşinari, ten miles west of Sibiu, nestling under the snow-covered foothills of the Fǎgǎraş Mountains. Here again, among the 6,000 people whose principal activity is raising cattle, was evidence

of the Transylvanian love of bright houses – coloured red, green,
blue or splashed with purple. We saw here Mrs Grecu Paraschiva,
a widow, aged seventy-four, whose parents had a large flock of
sheep. Immediately after she was married she had a cow which
used to give eight litres of milk a day but after a woman neigh-
hour, a *strigoaie,* had put a spell on it the yield dropped to three
litres a day and the calf almost died of hunger. She attributed
this witchcraft to the *strigoaie* who came to the courtyard early
one morning without any good reason. No one saw her come but
by the time Mrs Paraschiva got up the mischief had been done.
She was told that if she heated the chain which went round the
cow's neck until it was red the milk would come back but it did
not. She tried many other ways of getting the milk back but
without success.

'This shows there is nothing you can do against witchcraft,'
said the widow.

One day when cows were being collected to be driven to
different fields the witch passed through the middle of them and
was threatened with a whip by the cowherd who told her what
he would do if a cow lost milk because of her.

When a witch dies, said Mrs Paraschiva, and people talk about
her she still knows who is talking, so they say 'God keep the
stone in her mouth'.

Mr Boner said it must be acknowledged that a belief in witchcraft was prevalent in Transylvania 'until very lately', and he
knew one place where the Greek priest asserted that the bad
harvest was owing to the number of witches in the land, and
that it would not be better till they were exterminated. Reputed
witches who had died were disinterred and turned round in the
grave to destroy their spells. This, however, was over a century
ago, and, as we have seen, belief in witchcraft still lingers on in
Transylvania.

There are more women than men in Sibiu today which would
not be surprising if they conformed to the appearance of the
Saxon women described by Mrs Gerard ninety years ago. They
had, she said, rather good hair, indifferent complexions, narrow
shoulders, flat busts and gigantic feet. Their features, 'of a sadly

unfinished wooden appearance', reminded her of the figures out of a sixpenny Noah's ark – a tart remark indeed! Dr Starkie, who came to Sibiu more than forty years later, considered her judgement harsh. Many of the women were so fair and tall that they made him think of Scandinavian beauty rather than German. 'They all seemed to have the secret of a beautiful complexion – a rare quality today when women insist on painting up their faces into a universal mask', he said. Dr Starkie was enchanted by the beauty of the girls at Săliște, fourteen miles from Sibiu, called by him the singing town of the Romanians. Săliște is still renowned for the beauty of its women.

If Mrs Gerard could return to Sibiu today she would find the streets full of pretty girls, Romanian rather than Saxon. They still, as in Dr Starkie's time, use little make-up, and have remained addicted to mini skirts and dresses long after they had gone out of fashion in the West. Still, Western fashions are popular, particularly denim jeans when they can be obtained, and if girls cannot find what they want in the shops they make their own clothes.

Back in Sibiu from the villages I was fed with statistics. The first hospital in Romania was opened in Sibiu in the thirteenth century; it was the second town in Europe, after Vienna, to have a tramway; the first public library was opened there in 1300; the first public school in Romania ('public' is not used here in the sense of the British public school) was opened in Sibiu in the fourteenth century, and the first book in the Romanian language, a Lutheran catechism, was printed in Sibiu in 1554. No copies of this book exist today, but an entry in the town accounts showed that two florins were paid to Filip Pictor on 13 July 1554 for printing the Romanian catechism, so that there is no doubt that there was such a book and it may still come to light. Konrad Hass, who designed rockets to conquer the universe in 1529, came from Sibiu, as did Professor Herman Oberth, who made the first experiments with interplanetary rockets, on the soil of Romania, in 1934; indeed, Transylvania has made a significant contribution to the development of aviation.

I was told that the production in all sections of the economy in the Sibiu region, which has a population of nearly half a million, has been raised by more than 600 per cent since 1960, the number of employees has increased by 73 per cent, and the overall production per inhabitant has been raised by 414 per cent, which hardly accords with Mrs Gerard's description of the 'indolent charm and the drowsy poetry of this secluded land', even allowing for the noted industry of the Saxons, which today is being more than matched by that of the Romanians.

Dr Starkie found Sibiu to be 'sad and mysterious'. It must have been a sad place for Dracula and his family when they lived there during the winter of 1475–6. The atmosphere, from what we know of the Saxons, would have been hostile to them, and Dracula was in no position now to impose his will on others. He had his plans on how, with Hungarian help, to regain his throne, and this meant intense diplomatic activity. Little is known about certain periods of Dracula's life, particularly his captivity and marriage, but, as Florescu and McNally point out in their book *Dracula,* 'the 1474–6 period, particularly the years 1475 and 1476, presents the historian with rich documentation, mostly internal and diplomatic.' These letters, all precisely dated, the originals of which are in the archives of Braşov and Sibiu, emanate from such Transylvanian towns as Arghis, Turda, Mediaş, Stemt, Merghindel and Balcaciu. It is not known whether Dracula's wife and children accompanied him on these journeys through Transylvania; if they did it would have provided them with a welcome relief from the tediousness of life in Sibiu.

By February 1476 Dracula's hold on Transylvania was so firmly entrenched that Laiotă Basarab, the ruling prince of Wallachia, wrote to the citizens of Sibiu that he no longer considered himself as 'their friend' since Dracula was living among them. The Saxons must have had some doubts on this point as well, but Dracula, as a friend or foe, was a man to be feared, and there could be no question of expelling him from the town to placate the Wallachian ruler. Some of the fire must have died in Dracula during his long period of Hungarian captivity; he was no longer master of his own destiny and able to play Turk against Hungarian for his own immediate advantage. He was now firmly attached to Matthias Corvinus as an ally.

If the house where Dracula lived in the last year of his life could be traced it would be visited annually by thousands of visitors and probably declared a building of historic importance, which it certainly is. This information may yet come to light. Even so, to wander through the old parts of Sibiu, and to visit the church where the remains of his son are buried and where Dracula almost certainly worshipped, is to step into the past.

9 Cluj and tales from the mountains

Cluj, the capital of Transylvania and the centre with the largest population (218,703), has close links with the Dracula story. Matthias Corvinus, King of Hungary and Dracula's captor, was born here, probably on 23 February 1440. In the centre of a large square laid out with flower beds is the noble equestrian statue of King Matthias by John Fadrusz, a sculptor from Cluj. The model of this statue won first prize at an exhibition in Paris in 1896 at which one thousand such models were judged. The king is shown accepting the homage of political leaders of the time, among them being Stephen Báthory (not the same Stephen Báthory who later besieged Sighişoara), who led Dracula's ill-fated expedition to regain his throne in Wallachia.

The statue adjoins St Michael's Roman Catholic Church, one of the largest Gothic churches in Romania. Matthias Corvinus saw the church in the process of construction which lasted from 1350 to 1487. This church, which has suffered in all possible ways, now by fire, now by bombardment, explosions and by destroying hordes, is the only monument of the medieval city of Cluj where the visitor can still see parts of the original paintings of that time.

The house where Matthias Corvinus was born, built in a Gothic style in the first half of the fifteenth century, is the only one of that period still preserved. Additions have been made to it, the rectangular windows being added in the first decade of the sixteenth century as was the ample porch in a broken arch. The king also influenced the decision to build the reformed Church which still stands in Cluj.

The emphasis in Cluj on the reign of Matthias Corvinus means something more than local pride. According to the *Encyclopaedia*

Britannica, Matthias was 'indisputably the greatest man of his day, and one of the greatest monarchs who ever reigned. Like Napoleon, with whom he has often been compared, he was equally illustrious as a soldier, a statesman, an orator, a legislator and an administrator; but unlike him a fine moral character.' This reference to Matthias's moral character suggests that it is unlikely he would have allowed Dracula to marry into his family if he was as debased in his tastes as the Saxon-German chronicles suggest.

Matthias, who died in 1490, was for a time King of Bohemia. After he defeated the Austrian Emperor Frederick III in 1485 he established his capital in Vienna. Matthias was, as has already been pointed out, the son of Iancu of Hunedoara (John Hunyadi), and therefore of Romanian origin. Hunedoara Castle, south-west of Cluj, where Dracula and his father were probably guests, was presented to Iancu's father, Prince Voicu, by King Sigismund of Hungary as a reward for his valour. Both Iancu and Matthias Corvinus made great changes in the citadel, which became a beautiful castle, but when Boner saw it in 1863 it was a ruin, 'but still grand in its proportions, and imposing from its commanding and massy forms'.

He continued that

A fire broke out here in the night of 12 April 1854 in one of the towers, and spreading with fearful quickness, soon made the noble castle what it is now – a place of desolation. Here and there some roofing had been raised to prevent the rains from deluging the rooms; but beyond this, nothing has been done. There is one magnificent vaulted knightly hall, built 1452, with stone columns down its whole length : the damp and snow enter by the windows, and from above the wet penetrates and disintegrates the stone. Bit by bit, fragments loosen and fall down. It is a shame and pity that it should be so. Before long, it will crumble and be gone.

I quote this passage, because it is one of the seven references in the book to 'monuments spoiled and neglected'. The Hungarian authorities at that time did not appreciate the historic importance of many buildings in Transylvania. Boner points out that when the emperor visited Hunedoara Castle (the date is not given) the walls were plastered over with mortar and then whitewashed. 'Let us fancy the walls and round tower of Windsor, Belvoir or Edinburgh castles being treated in this way,' he remarked.

Fortunately, Hunedoara Castle, which has fifty rooms, some decorated with mural paintings, has recently been restored. When I visited the castle I was shown a well ninety feet deep on which three Turkish prisoners worked for fifteen years having been promised freedom if they struck water. They succeeded, but in the meantime the governor of the castle had died, and his promise was not honoured by his successor. In despair the Turks wrote on the wall adjoining the well, 'You have water but no souls.'

In the battlements there is a pit in which, according to oral tradition, Turkish prisoners who were not strong enough to work fought with lions while noblemen looked on from above, a strange revival of a practice common in Roman times.

Unlike most castles in Europe, Hunedoara overlooks a grim industrial scene, but one with its own beauty, the chimneys in the iron and steel complex belching forth smoke varying in colour from orange to pale grey. When you stand in the finest room in the castle, the hall of knights, you see buckets of ore being winched across the valley – a contrast indeed. If Dracula could stand on the battlements today he would stare at the scene with astonishment and awe, just as he would at the hydro-electric power station below his citadel in the Argeş Valley.

Cluj, incidentally, is one of the few places in Transylvania where the paths of a principal character in Bram Stoker's novel, the young solicitor Jonathan Harker, and the historical Dracula cross. Stoker brings Harker from Budapest to Klausenburg, the German name for Cluj (the Hungarian one is Koloszvár), where he stopped the night at the Hotel Royale, having for dinner, or rather supper, 'a chicken done up some way with red pepper, which was very good but thirsty'. The industrious Professor Wolf, researching for his *Annotated Dracula*, tried to find a listing of the Hotel Royale in his *Baedeker* of the time, but without success, remarking 'Why Harker, as a patriotic Englishman, did not stay in the *Königin von England* (Queen of England) is a puzzle'. It is probable that Bram Stoker consulted

Boner's book in the course of his research, and there he would
have seen that 'There is a large hotel at Klausenburg, well kept,
neat, clean, and orderly. It is probably the best in Transylvania.'
However, Boner kept the name of this inn to himself, so that the
author of *Dracula,* not bothering to turn to a guide book, settled
on the Hotel Royale as a name suggesting a certain degree of
opulence and standing.

Cluj was originally a Saxon town, but the Germans began to
leave it on religious grounds in 1540 and later it was a strongly
Hungarian centre and a winter resort for the nobility. Cluj is
now known officially as Cluj-Napoca. The Dacian city which
stood on this site was known as Napoca – it was mentioned by
Ptolemy in the second century BC – and the name was retained
by the Romans when they raised the settlement to the rank of
municipality, and it became the capital of the province of Dacia
Porolissensis. At a ceremony in Michael the Brave Square
attended by 100,000 people of the district in 1974 to mark the
1,850th anniversary of the city, President Nicolae Ceauşescu
signed the decree which gave the city of Cluj the name of Cluj-
Napoca 'in order to perpetuate the name of this age-old settlement, a testimony to the seniority and continuity of the Romanian
people in these parts.'

Those travellers in the past from whose books I have quoted,
Mrs Gerard and Dr Starkie, enjoyed themselves in Cluj, finding
it livelier than Sibiu. Dr Starkie listened to Hungarians and
Romanians who made counter claims to Transylvania. The city
then possessed two distinct societies, one Hungarian and the
other Romanian, 'and hardly a member of either knows anyone
of the opposite faction.' Dr Starkie's conclusion was that

Transylvania has always been separate from Hungary in its
traditions, though the Magyars were in the ascendancy; it has
always been a centre of toleration and religious liberty in comparison to other parts of the country. . . . And now after centuries of
Magyar rule the country has returned to its original rulers, the
Romanians, the descendants of the Dacians who were incorporated
in Trajan's Empire. It will be instructive to watch the effect of the
Romanian government's policy in the next ten years. I know of no

more interesting struggle than that which is taking place in Transylvania between the culture of the Magyars and the culture of the Romanians. What will happen to Cluj in our modern age? Will it go the way of so many old European cities that have had to accept modern progress?

It is possible now to answer in part Dr Starkie's question 'What will happen to Cluj in our modern age?' Life, although more sophisticated than it was, is still leisurely outside working hours. When you look from your hotel window in any large centre in Romania between six and seven in the morning you see neatly dressed people bustling to work, but by late afternoon the day at the office or factory is over and the cafés are crowded. In Cluj's Liberty Square, where the statue of Matthias Corvinus stands, students are devouring fried sausages bought at a snack bar and housewives are bustling home with bags filled from shops which line the square. Some pause to discuss the day's news over a coffee and an 'ischler', the famous Vienna cake. Elderly men, with a coffee or beer on the table in front of them, linger as long over a newspaper as they might in Paris. The fierce late afternoon sun makes one disinclined for exertion. The atmosphere of what Dr Starkie called 'the Oxford of the East of Europe, with its students and its traditional buildings', remains much as it was when he was in Cluj nearly fifty years ago.

The answer to Dr Starkie's other question, that of Romanian-Hungarian relations in Transylvania, is more complex, and involves other questions that had not been raised in his time. The population of 21,142,000 in Romania includes nearly two million Hungarian speakers, most of them resident in Transylvania, which has a population of five and a half millions. Dr Starkie saw the situation in Transylvania as a struggle between the culture of the Magyars and that of the Romanians, but this seems to me to be an over simplification. Neither side could win such a struggle, particularly as the Hungarians account for over one-fifth of the population of Transylvania. Hungarians in Transylvania are Romanian citizens and no attempt has been made to deprive them of their national culture. I had the opportunity to study the so-called Hungarian problem in Transylvania some years ago before making the present series of visits to collect material on folk beliefs. The conclusion I reached then, and I see no reason to abandon it now, is that the Hungarian minority is not victimized in any way. In the famous Babeş-Bolyai University in Cluj, representing a merger of an older Romanian university with a Hungarian university formed in 1945, I have seen Hungarian students being taught in their own language in 77 out of the total of 207 courses. Younger pupils are also taught in their native Hungarian. Hungarians have their own theatres, including an opera house at Cluj, six drama theatres, and can buy books, newspapers and magazines in Hungarian; for instance 216 books in Hungarian were published in 1975 compared with 187 in 1970. New industries have been set up in centres where Hungarians predominate. The Hungarians have twenty-nine members in the Grand National Assembly out of a total of 349; the Germans have eight members, and other nationalities are also represented.

The Saxons, too, have the same minority rights as the Hungarians, as have other minorities, but the German descendants of the early settlers do not have the same commercial dominance as before. They now comprise only 2 per cent of the entire population. After the war Romanian citizens of German descent were, in general, allowed to emigrate, and 200,000, or nearly one third of the country's German-speaking population, left the country. Descendants of French and Swiss settlers were similarly allowed to emigrate, but emigration was no more an answer to the problem of the presence of the Hungarians in Transylvania than it has been to the problem of people of Anglo-Scottish descent in Northern Ireland when Irish unity is discussed.

There is no doubt that anti-Romanian feeling exists among Hungarian emigrés who, for sentimental reasons, still regard Transylvania as belonging to them. In 1975 the opposition to Romania's attempt to obtain most-favoured nation treatment in its trade relations with the United States came almost entirely from members of the Hungarian lobby in Congress who claimed that there was discrimination against Hungarians in Transylvania. This opposition was not allowed to prevail, however. Rather

more serious is the Soviet Union's use of the Hungarian
'problem' in Transylvania as a threat to Romanian independence
of action in international issues. Alone of the countries whose
armed forces compose the Warsaw pact, Romania did not take
part in the occupation of Czechoslovakia in 1968. It was also the
only member of the East European Bloc to maintain diplomatic
relations with Israel after the outbreak of hostilities with the
Arab countries. The Russians have been angered by this and by
Romania's independent economic policy. In addition to putting
economic pressure on Romania the Russians, who have been
ruthless in suppressing nationalism in their own minorities, have
been applying political pressure by encouraging Hungarian
nationalism, including the political aspirations of Hungarians in
Transylvania.

No one can visit Hungary, as I have, without forming a great
attachment to the spirited and talented people there. An earlier
traveller, Charles Boner, also had a great regard for the Hungarians, but he was not sympathetic to their viewpoint when he
discussed Hungarian-Austrian relations in regard to Transylvania
after his visit there in 1863.

With the Hungarian, every question becomes crystalized into one
of nationality : this warps his judgement, for he thus regards even
those which are most diverging from one sole special point of view.
Argument is then at an end, and a rabid state begins. . . . Owing to
this extreme party feeling, the Hungarian is not at all reliable in
his statement of a case; circumstances which tell against him are
left out altogether. All relate their story in one way, and keep to it.
They do not observe the same honesty in dealing with political
questions as they would consider themselves bound to do in transactions of social life. Like Lord Bacon, in his explanations of natural
phenomena, they presuppose certain conditions which are to their
purpose, and having posed these, argue accordingly. Consequently,
the version given is rather in accordance with the presupposition
than with the reality. The Hungarian loves especially to dwell on
the ' historische Standpunkt ' – to take his stand on history. Against
this nothing is allowed to have weight : neither civilization, culture
nor expediency. On the other hand, however, he does not heed the
' historische Standpunkt ' when it tells against his wishes. The fact

that Transylvania was definitely separated from Hungary when it fell to Austria is disregarded. Because, before that, the countries belonged together, and because he would wish the addition, in order that Hungary may be aggrandized, the Hungarian demands that they shall be so considered now.

Charles Boner writes here as if the Hungarians were the original rulers of Transylvania, but the Romanians maintain, rightly in my opinion, that they were the first rulers, and the country became Hungarian only by conquest and even then retained a special status. Still, as the journalist Paul Neuburg pointed out in *The Guardian* of 29 July 1974, Eastern Europe is in fact riddled with minority problems and the minorities themselves invariably feel discriminated against. 'But useful as Eastern European minority problems are to Moscow in exerting pressure through non-military means, any fierce airing of the issue in the area would be very much against Russia's interests. The Soviet Union's own minority and nationality problems, if they were ever really opened, could form a tinder box.'

Quite obviously there is less tension now between Romanians and Hungarians than there was nearly fifty years ago when Dr Starkie was in Transylvania, and, if left to themselves, no problems should arise. Romania has nothing like the racial problems that exist in neighbouring Yugoslavia.

It is time to return to the highways and byways in search of folk beliefs, which is the main reason that I went to Transylvania. I was fortunate to have Professor Ioan A. Popa, of the Department of English at Cluj University, as interpreter and guide to the western Carpathians, particularly as he had relatives in the district. Our first visit was to the tiny village of Lunca Arieşului (population 379) thirty miles west of Cluj, skirting the eastern side of the range on the way. The scenery here was reminiscent of the Highlands of Scotland, but it was grander and more rugged when we crossed a bridge over the river Arieş and bumped along a rough track into the village, which was overlooked by crags, some wooded and others just slabs of rock, of a height of 3,600 feet.

I had been warned that I must not expect too much from such

a visit to a village which had not been arranged in advance; it was always possible that no old person with tales of former days still lived there. We had to rely on the knowledge of the local priest for this, and all too often he alone could persuade an old villager to speak of his or her experiences to a stranger from the West. The *popa* and his wife were not at home – he had been attending a meeting at a neighbouring centre, we were told – so that we settled down to wait. The sun had set, shadows from the crags lengthened over the landscape, and as it was still early spring there was a chill in the air.

The *popa's* wife was the first to arrive. Being told of my mission, she invited us to her husband's study, which was soon warmed when she lit the stove. The priest, Ioan Voica, a handsome man of sixty, his dark hair fringed with white, arrived shortly afterwards. He had been priest there since 1940, he explained, and his parish embraced three villages. Most of the people worked on a co-operative farm eighteen miles away, travelling there by train and bus. Others worked in forestry or on railway construction.

While we sipped very strong home-made plum brandy (*ţuică*) – the glass of a guest is never left empty for long – the priest explained that all the people in the village belonged to the Orthodox faith, but religious belief was not as strong as it was fifty years ago. He knew of the custom of putting embers in water as protection against the evil eye, and that red tassels were placed on oxen for the same purpose; the practice, however, now being mainly for ornament.

In the meantime the *popa's* wife had been busy. The dark world of the mountains was shut out while the stove burned and the *ţuică* flowed. A religious – or anti-religious – disputation broke out in a corner, but as it was in Romanian I was not involved. I was now to experience true Transylvanian hospitality. Home-made smoked pork sausages were served with bread and then smoked pork fat eaten with raw onions, a pleasant and homely dish although in cold print it may not seem particularly appetizing. This was followed by the national dish of *sarmale*, made of pork and beef mixed together in soured cabbage leaves with cream on top of it, washed down with home-made rosé wine.

In the darkened village the *popa* led me by the arm to the cottage of Lucăiana Chirilă, a former midwife, aged ninety-five. Having been warned of my visit while we ate, she sat in her bed awaiting us, a frail figure with a black scarf around her head. Mrs Chirilă, who was born near here, said that her first husband died in 1918, leaving her with five children, and her second husband in 1963.

When she was young people believed that ghosts were all around, Mrs Chirilă stated, and it was generally accepted that you would not leave your home on a Tuesday night because of ghosts. Why Tuesday? She did not know, but old people said then that if you went out on a Tuesday night things would happen to you and she would certainly not go out on that night. I looked into this point later. Marcu Beza says in his *Paganism in Roumanian Folklore* that popular tradition throws back the creation to about 5,500 BC and it is believed to have commenced on a Tuesday. Therefore one must not proceed on a journey, get married or start anything on that particular day. Such refraining is expressed in two characteristic proverbs: 'As if he were born on a Tuesday' is said about an unlucky man; 'All things upside down and the wedding on a Tuesday', when all is going wrong. Mrs Gerard says that 'About sunset on Tuesday the evil spirit of that day is at its fullest force, and many people refrain from leaving their huts between sunset and midnight. "May the *mar sara (marţi seara)* – the spirit of Tuesday evening – carry you off!" is here equivalent to saying "May the devil take you!"'

Mrs Chirilă said that when she was four or five years old an old woman looked at her and praised her skirt. Her mouth closed and she had to be carried home, where her mother opened her mouth with a spoon. I interpreted this as the effects of the evil eye. Only those people who had the evil eye looked at the priest when he came out of the altar at the end of the service, said Mrs Chirilă; all the other members of the congregation looked down.

When she was young she remembered seeing a woman walking

among cows, marking their hind legs and cutting the hair on them with scissors. She did this because she wanted to take the milk away. It so happened that the milk from these cows was very weak. She personally saw this but other people did not.

Mrs Chirilă told the priest that when she was young red tassels and other red objects were placed on animals to ward off the evil eye (on our arrival in the village we had seen a team of oxen with red tassels fixed to their horns pulling a cart). She remembered that years ago when she was at a burial loud thunder was heard and an old woman attributed this sound to ghosts. In her youth she was accustomed to hearing stories about werewolves. 'Everyone believed them. Werewolves are the real *strigoii*', she stated.

Another memory of Mrs Chirilă's childhood was of hearing magic incantations when herbs were used to cure illness. Mrs Chirilă spoke with fervour and the utmost conviction. I was sorry to leave Lunca Arieşului and the friendly *popa* and his wife for the bright lights of the modern hotel at Cluj. I did not know then that I was to meet an even older woman the following day.

Maria Costea is the oldest woman I have seen or am likely to see. She lives in the mountain village of Mătiseşti at a height of nearly 5,000 feet, and to meet her I had travelled nearly a hundred miles south-west from Cluj. Mrs Costea is uncertain of her age. I was told she was 110, but she had with her a son, Traian Costea, who is sixty-seven, and he said that he was born when his mother was forty-six, so that she could have been 113. Three of her twelve children are still alive. She had never travelled far from her village.

Maria Costea is a little shrivelled woman, toothless, her head covered with a cloth. The local *popa* had led the way up the hillside to her barely furnished cottage. Two years ago her hearing and her eyesight deteriorated severely. Conversation was conducted in shouts, mainly by the *popa*, who, understandably, acted as intermediary in this meeting with strangers. At times her memory flickered into remembering events of the past, but most had been forgotten and could not be recalled.

'What do you know about ghosts?' the priest shouted.

The son joined in, recollecting something his mother had told him. When there was a heavy snowstorm they would say that the *strigoi* had died and this had disturbed the weather.

When this was related to Mrs Costea she nodded in agreement. Her memory came briefly to life. Yes, she believed in witchcraft. She remembered that once she milked a cow in the barn and before she reached the house the milk was sour. This was due to witchcraft and those who had performed it would do so by sticking a knife in the attic of the barn to take away the cow's milk.

Mrs Costea could not remember hearing of a body being staked in the grave to prevent the corpse from becoming a *strigoi*. 'It is a sin to speak of something one has not seen,' she added.

The mother and son spoke of an old woman they remembered who, when a snowstorm was coming, would stick an axe in the threshold of a house and utter incantations to keep the storm away. Did this work? Yes, the snow would start falling and then slacken off. In his piping voice the son imitated the old woman's incantation. His niece, aged ten, who had arrived from school while this conversation was taking place, listened wide-eyed to the talk of ghosts. Remote as this village of 840 people is, it has television, and these tales of witches, ghosts and incantations against snowstorms must have puzzled the little girl.

The account of the old woman with her axe and incantations reminded me of a somewhat similar story in Mrs Gerard's book. In it she says that 'many years ago, in the village of Wermesch, there lived a peasant who, whenever a thunderstorm was seen approaching, used to take his stand in front of it, armed with an axe, by which means he always turned the storm aside.' Wermesch, now known as Vermeş, is near Bistriţa.

Our original destination had been the village of Albac, but the priest there was conducting a service and his wife suggested that we should visit Mătişeşti and then return. We travelled along an abominable road that was under repair. The driver, twisting and turning between the puddles and ruts, could progress only at a snail's pace; indeed, a less resolute one would have turned back – the exhaust pipe was later found to be fractured. Then the icy road turned upwards and was fortunately free of repairs. Children coming out of school stared wonderingly at the strangers, but my eyes were caught by the vista of snow-covered hills dotted with cottages. Here we were in the *ţara moţilor,* the country of the Mots, as the local inhabitants are called, doughty fighters in the famous Transylvanian revolutions.

Back in Albac we had a late lunch with the *popa,* Iuliu Todea, who said that when he arrived there as priest forty-six years ago his parishioners believed in witchcraft. Some still believed that milk could be taken from the cow by witchcraft, 'but ninety per cent have stopped believing in *strigoii* and that sort of thing.' The priest explained through Dr Popa, who had also acted as interpreter at Mătiseşti, that the only folk belief which had really survived in the village was that if someone committed suicide bad weather would follow.

When Charles Boner was in Transylvania over a century ago he formed a poor opinion of the Romanian priests because all too often they were illiterate, sometimes drunken, and one or two were noted thieves. At one place where he stayed the priest worked daily with the other peasantry, from whom he was not to be distinguished by dress or anything else. In another village the people told him that they had turned their *popa* away; he was such an incorrigible drunkard that they could not have him any longer. An acquaintance related how, once seeing a number of men lay hold of a person who struggled to get free, he asked what was the matter, and received for answer 'This is the priest, and as today is Saturday we are going to lock him up till tomorrow, so that he may keep sober; for if we do not he will be so tipsy in the morning as to be unable to read the service. When church is over, we shall let him go again.' Boner considered that the priests, 'grossly ignorant as they are, become the ready instruments of those placed above them, and, in their turn, exercise great influence on all followers of their creed. In political matters they are powerful allies; so implicit is the obedience exacted and rendered.'

The position today is, of course, greatly different. No doubt any congregation, particularly in villages, contains a fairish proportion of elderly semi-literate peasants, but the *popa* is now well educated and interested in events of the wider world, as are many in his congregation. In many Transylvanian villages the priest has to share the life and interests of the peasants, although he no longer works daily in the fields with them. A scholar more or less confined to his study when he was not taking services could hardly fill a pastoral role. For instance, the *popa* at Albac told me that he had to be prepared to go by horse on a journey that could last up to two and a half hours if any parishioner needed his help. I was impressed by the type of man found in the priesthood in present-day Romania.

The journey to Albac had been through countryside unfamiliar to most tourists. Here again there was evidence, as in a church painted blue or the silver cupolas on buildings, of the love of Transylvanians for colour. I was intrigued to see in a churchyard a pole decorated with fir, ribbons and baubles. This was not for some festive occasion but to mark the burial of an unmarried person. The *popa* explained that when unmarried people die a fir tree is placed by the cross in the cemetery. On our return journey we passed a funeral procession with banners and twigs of fir on the coffin. Thus there has been little change since Boner was in Transylvania, where he found that 'In the village churchyards were sometimes six or eight tall saplings, twenty feet high, over a grave, all the branches and bark stripped off, with merely a tuft of foliage at the top; these indicated that a youth lay buried beneath.'

In Albac we were in a village bordering the Apuseni Mountains, the most highly populated of Romanian mountains, from which the Dacians mined most of their gold, the Romans later exploiting the workings. When the nobles of the district opposed the decree of the Emperor Joseph II of Austria abolishing all personal servitude for serfs, the peasant rising of 1784 took place led by Nicolae Horia, who came from Albac, and Cloşca and Crişan, three resolute peasants from the Apuseni Mountains. In a fews days the revolt had spread all over western Transylvania and many of the manors of the Hungarian nobles were burned to the ground. Some Hungarian serfs joined the uprising and so did the two Magheru brothers, Wallachians of Transylvanian descent. Although the rising was finally put down and its leaders executed (Horia and Cloşca were put to the terrible torture of the wheel; Crişan, knowing what awaited him, killed himself in prison and the Magheru brothers were put to death), 'it was not nevertheless barren of results', according to Professor Giurescu in his *Transylvania in the History of Romania.*

The 1848 revolution came at a time much more opportune for change and was much more broadly based in its appeal. When Boner was in Transylvania fifteen years after the resolution was suppressed with fierce fighting there was still much evidence of the sacking and pillaging that took place then. According to Boner, the Hungarian nobles had neglected their estates and were in part responsible for what followed: 'instead of caring for their property, or taking on themselves the duty of their station, they acted the part of the Irish absentees. They did nothing for the country, but gave a bad example of wastefulness and neglect.' After the revolution, however, they did much to improve their estates. A noted fighter in the people's struggle in 1848–9 was the young *moţ*, Avram Iancu. Masses of armed peasants then made the Apuseni Mountains a veritable stronghold.

To most tourists the Apuseni Mountains are best known for the Maidens' Fair (or Market) held on the plateau of Mount Găina on the Sunday nearest 20 July, although a century ago all the marriageable girls for miles around used to assemble there to be courted on 29 June, the feast of St Peter and St Paul. Although this fair is the best known, maidens' fairs are held in various parts of the country. Jules Verne described one held near Uricani, which was then a village but is now a town in the Petroşani depression:

Every year, at the feast of St Peter, there opens ' the fair of the betrothed'. On that day all the marriageable girls of the district are assembled. They come in their best carriages drawn by their best horses; they bring with them their dowry, that is to say, the clothes they have spun, and sewn, and embroidered with their hands, and these are all packed in gaudily coloured boxes; their relatives and women friends and neighbours accompanying them. And then the young men arrive dressed in their best clothes and girt with silken sashes; proudly they strut through the fair; they choose the girl they take a fancy to; they give her a ring and a handkerchief in token of betrothal, and the marriages take place at the close of the fair.

This sounds a very casual way of getting married and the reality behind the meetings at these fairs was rather different. According to Emily Gerard, who presumably attended the fair on Mount Găina in the 1880s,

The trousseau, packed in a gaily decorated chest, was placed in a cart harnessed with the finest horses or the fattest oxen, and thus the girl and her whole family proceeded to the place of rendezvous. Sheep, calves, poultry and even beehives were likewise brought by way of decoration; and many people went to the length of borrowing cattle or furniture in order to cut a better figure and lure on the suitors – although it was an understood thing that only a part of what was thus displayed really belonged to the maiden's dowry. The destination being reached, each family having a girl to dispose of erected its tent, with the objects grouped around, and seated in front was the head of the family, smoking his pipe and awaiting the suitors. The young men on their side came also accompanied by their families, bringing part of their property with them, notably a broad leather belt well stocked with gold and silver coins. When an agreement had been effected, then the betrothal took place on the spot, with music, dancing and singing, and it hardly ever happened that a girl returned home unbetrothed from this meeting. But, to say the truth, this was, latterly, only because each girl attending the fair went there virtually betrothed to some youth with whom all the preliminaries of courtship had already been gone through, and this was merely the official way of celebrating the betrothal – the Romanians in these parts believing that good luck will only attend such couples as are affianced in this manner.

Mrs Gerard, pointing out that any girl who had not got a bridegroom in sight, rarely went there at all, or, if she did, did not take her trousseau, but considered herself as a mere spectator, said that in former days this assemblage had a real significance and was dictated by a real necessity. There were fewer villages, and a far larger proportion than now of the population led the wandering nomadic life of mountain shepherds, cut off from intercourse with their fellow creatures during the greater part of the year, and with no opportunity of making choice of a consort.

The Maidens' Fair on Mount Găina is hardly a marriage market these days, as there are plenty of other opportunities for young men and women to meet, but it continues as a festival to perpetuate the tradition of the fair, which is centuries old. The Romanians are fond of festivals, some of which are in honour of historical events, but in the main they are occasions on which songs, dances and the costumes of the region are presented. One such festival, the Cherry Fair at Brîncoveneşti, in Mureş County, was formerly a maidens' fair, but in the course of time it has changed into a popular festival with the folklore groups of the county, and from the Hargita and Bistriţa-Năsăud counties, participating in it.

Incantations, we have seen, are still remembered by older people in the mountains. Some fascinating material collected in the Sebeş Valley, forty miles north-west of Sibiu, between 1934 and 1939 is presented by Dr Pavelescu in a pamphlet on medical folklore published in Cluj in 1974.

The main role of an incantation is as a 'verbal sedative' through suggestion, says Dr Pavelescu, and in illness strongly affected by the mental condition of the patient, the incantation develops in a chromatic monotone 'which probably has a psycho-physical action'.

An incantation collected by Robert Prexl in the vicinity of Sebeş in the last century for the treatment of depression is a poem of almost seventy lines containing images developing the sensation of darkness: 'they took two black men; two black axes and put them on two black shoulders. They departed on a black road, went to a black wood and departed on the black road and came to the black court. . . .'

An incantation for relieving headaches brings in constant references to green: 'A green man takes a green axe, goes to the green forest and cuts off a green tree', while for inflammation of the gums the recurring word is red : 'The red man with the red axe goes to the red forest and cuts red wood. . . .'

Dr Pavelescu comments that 'the extraordinarily chromatic imagination of the incantations seems to have sometimes a psycho-therapeutic role'.

The prescription for defending cows against ghosts is interesting, says Dr Pavelescu. For this purpose one bores through a horn, usually the right one, then corks it up after putting inside gold, wax, incense, myrrh, spring wheat and garlic, 'bacterial volatile substances to defend the cow against microbes, the invisible enemies' (the use of gold suggests to me that shepherds were able to obtain it in small quantities from mountain streams; a highway running through the valley climbs towards the Şurean and Cibin Mountains).

Among the folk remedies mentioned by Dr Pavelescu are coal in the form of embers, good for indigestion ('the evil eye'), basil and garlic for stomach ulcers; honey for erysipelas, and milk for washing poisonous wounds. He says that 'it is possible that future discoveries in medicine and biochemistry should increase the interest of researchers in some practices of our folk medicine'.

Dr Pavelescu states that in the mountain villages of the Sebeş and Pian valleys, south of the Alba area, a rich and interesting folk art of a pastoral type was preserved until the first decades of the nineteenth century. The very ancient elements of this culture, some dating from the Dacian period and others possibly from the neolithic one, were enriched throughout the centuries from sources beyond the Carpathians by the movement of flocks. Many of the beliefs and practices met with in the Sebeş area proved to have been known in antiquity, beginning with the ancient inhabitants of India, then the Greeks and Romans, as well as in some modern races such as the French, Italians, Germans, Scots and Norwegians.

Among the medical practices having a magical aspect which have been preserved in a few villages in the Sebeş area the most widespread is the 'rose' prescription for erysipelas practised in the villages of Răchita and Sebeşel. For this prescription the initials of Jesus Christ set in reverse are written in Cyrillic characters within the framework of a cross. The paper with this inscription is smeared with honey and laid on the sufferer from erysipelas. Those practising this remedy are aware of the therapeutic value of the honey, yet the treatment has a lot of magical elements, according to Dr Pavelescu.

The prescription is to be written only by old people whose power decreases, with the left hand and inverted letters, so that the 'rose' (ie the patch of red skin) should regress. After twenty-four hours (in Sebeşel) and three days (in Răchita) the prescription is taken off the 'rose' before sunset, wrapped round a small stone, and taken to running water. His back turned to the water, the sick man genuflects three times, throws the paper into the water, and thrice says 'It is the rose I have thrown into the water, not the paper'.

During this time the sufferer must not look back nor speak to anyone. Dr Pavelescu says that the 'rose' prescription, which has been preserved in old books and in breviaries or prayer books, was probably brought, with the movement of flocks, from south of the Carpathians.

Dr Pavelescu states that a prescription for the treatment of rabies found in Răchita uses as an incantation formula the well-known Sator palindrome (*'Sator arepo tenet opera rotas'*). This formula, written on two pieces of wood from the lime tree, is more than 200 years old and was brought, according to tradition, from Mount Athos in Greece.

The inscription is imprinted on nine flat cakes made of unsifted saltless spring flour that has not risen when baked on the kitchen range. The heads of Spanish flies are put inside the cakes. The man suffering from rabies eats the cakes by taking them in his mouth from a window ledge: in this way he avoids touching them. Before washing himself the sufferer must eat three cakes a morning for three days, nine cakes in all.

Victoria Cetină, of Răchita, who still preserves pieces of wood containing the incantation formula, told Dr Pavelescu in 1971 that she had seen a man suffering from rabies cured of the illness after following the treatment prescribed by her grandmother, Maria Tot, who died in 1943 at the age of eighty-three.

The peasants who used this formula for rabies could hardly have been aware of how dangerous it was. According to the *Encyclopedia Americana,* 'Perhaps the most dangerous drug employed as an aphrodisiac was Cantharides (Spanish flies) consisting of dried beetles of the species *Cantharis Vesicatoria.* This substance is extremely irritating when applied to the skin; taken internally it acts as a powerful irritant on the genito-urinary tract, causing difficulty in urinating, excrutiating pain, and bloody urine. As little as 1.5 grams have proved fatal.'

The use of incantations against rabies is not confined to Romania and neighbouring countries in the Balkans. A paragraph in The Londoner's Diary in the *Evening Standard* of 5 October 1976 said that an anti-rabies ring was sold at Christie's, the auctioneers, for £310. Protection against mad dogs was guaranteed if the wearer recited the seventeenth-century magic charm, DABY HABY HABER HEBR. The columnist remarked 'If you have not got £310, avoid mad dogs'.

10 Bistrița and folk customs in the valleys

When Bram Stoker, researching in the British Museum, decided to bring Jonathan Harker to Count Dracula's castle near the Bîrgău (Borgo) Pass it was obvious that he had to be accommodated *en route* in the ancient town of Bistrița in north-eastern Transylvania. The Count had even selected the hotel where he should stay, 'The Golden Crown', which Harker found, to his great delight, to be 'thoroughly old fashioned'. In view of the horrors to come in the Count's castle this was just as well, but Bistrița at that time was ill-served by its inns.

Bistrița was a Saxon town, where the principal inn, the '*Stadt Wirthshaus*', belonged to the municipality, and Charles Boner records that there was no town in Transylvania with a worse conducted inn than the '*Stadt Wirthshaus*' in Bistrița. 'The business is, in fact, not conducted at all; everything goes on in a happy-go-lucky style, no one in the house caring anything about it. Neither master nor mistress trouble themselves about the matter; and while I was there the little Jew waiter, when at home, did nothing but smoke or lie down on his bed. Dirt and disorder prevailed.' The reason for this sad state of affairs, Boner remarked, was that Saxons were hardly ever inn keepers, looking on the occupation as being beneath them, so that the business, therefore, was in the hands of Bohemians, Poles and others 'whose habits as regards neatness and order leave much to be desired'. Mr Boner attributed the state of the inns then to the paucity of travellers, and consequently of demand for good accommodation. The position now is entirely different; the hotels are of a good standard.

There was no 'Golden Crown' hotel in Bistrița in Stoker's day, Professor Wolf discovered in his research for his *Annotated*

F

Dracula (the novelist seems to have drawn on his imagination
for the names of inns in certain localities, as he has done also in
placing the historical Dracula's Castle in north-eastern Transylvania), but there is a 'Golden Crown' hotel in Bistriţa today, a
fine modern building with 110 rooms, opened in April 1974 to
cater for the fast-developing Dracula industry, which is not, of
course, confined to Transylvania.

Professor Alexandru Misiuga, Director of the National Tourist
Office for the Bistriţa-Năsăud district, is a keen Dracula fan and
one of the two Romanian citizens who have been made honorary
life members of the Dracula Society. There is a painting of the
fictional Dracula in his office, where we drank with him Elixir
Dracula, a red liqueur (what other colour would be suitable?)
made from plums. He took us to the shop in the hotel where
souvenirs for visiting Dracula enthusiasts are sold. Here you can
buy a portrait of Christopher Lee as Count Dracula painted on
glass, paintings of Dracula, his eyes staring wildly, on bottles and
bowls, a Dracula plum brandy, 60 per cent alcohol, and, sur-
prisingly, salami made from bear meat mixed with that of the
wild boar. This particular salami is not on sale in any other shop
in the country; the price of £2.50 reflects its rarity value.

I was told that there are more bears in the vicinity of Bistriţa
than in any other part of the country. Boner, a keen sportsman,
mentioned that at Kushmar (now Cuşma), in the neighbourhood
of Bistriţa, about five bears were shot annually. There was no
question then (in 1863) of bears being slaughtered in large
numbers. 'One gentleman, who is perhaps the most noted
sportsman in Transylvania, has shot but eight in his life, a
number which, considering his age, his perseverance, and his
skill, is certainly not large.' I am told that very few bears are
shot today.

Before Jonathan Harker left Bistriţa he dined at the 'Golden
Crown' on 'what they call "robber steak" – bits of bacon, onion
and beef seasoned with red pepper, and strung on sticks and
roasted over the fire, in the simple style of the London's cat
meat! The wine was golden Mediasch, which produces a queer
sting on the tongue, which is, however, not disagreeable.'

Professor Misiuga has on these few culinary hints compiled a luncheon menu for members of the Dracula societies on tour consisting of the Elixir Dracula, sandwich with bear salami, 'outlaws' roast beef, smoked bacon with onions, 'butcher's' meat with pepper, and two glasses of golden Mediaș wine. The menu for dinner has been varied to include stuffed cabbages 'Bîrgău', Dracula cakes and Dracula red wine.

Professor Wolf was puzzled by the reference to the Golden Mediasch wine and made inquiries about it among experts in Cluj, but said that 'it continues to elude research'. If he had consulted Boner's book, however, he would have discovered that wine from Mediasch (Mediaș) was awarded the first prize, the great gold medal, at an exhibition at Munich. The jury there, 'while they adjudged the large gold medal to the Mediasch wine, could not help remarking on the poverty of the outward appliances, and the remembrance of the medicine and old ink-bottles in which it came excites still no little mirth.' The adjective 'golden' seems to have been added by Bram Stoker without good reason; wines from Mediasch, according to Boner, are 'very clear, light-coloured'.

Mediaș, a picturesque old town of 60,000 people surrounded by hills and renowned for its vineyards – the emblem of the town is a rich bunch of grapes – has links with the historical Dracula. It is known that after Dracula's capture the royal Hungarian party reached Mediaș on 11 December 1462, and correspondence reveals that he visited the town after his freedom was restored to him. However, there are no links with Bistrița, as far as is known, although Dracula may have stayed in the citadel which Iancu of Hunedoara (John Hunyadi) built there at the beginning of the fifteenth century. This citadel was destroyed after 1463 and subsequently rebuilt and fortified with towers, bastions, gates and ditches; vestiges are still to be seen today. We know that Dracula lived at Suceava, the capital of Moldavia, from December 1448 until October 1451 in the company of his cousin Stephen, the future Stephen the Great, so that it is possible that during that time he made an excursion to Bistrița.

It would be appropriate to the Dracula story if Bistriţa were situated in bleak windswept countryside but it is not; this is a region of orchards and vineyards, set in history. Celtic remains have been found here, and throughout the centuries it has been beset by sackings and fires. Bistriţa has nothing of the medieval look which distinguishes other former Saxon towns in Transylvania because it has been swept so often by fire; from 1836 to 1850 there were five conflagrations in which 325 houses were destroyed. Its nearness to the frontier exposed it to the devastations of Mongols and Tartars. One third of the inhabitants were killed by the plague in 1554, and when the town was besieged in 1602 for twenty days the foe before the walls and famine and disease within carried off 13,000 of the inhabitants. Bistriţa was nevertheless a prosperous town, a great mart for eastern trade, and fortunes were quickly restored, so that in 1560, only six years after the plague, the Saxons set about building their large church which still remains; the tower, nearly 230 feet high, is the highest in Romania. The Orthodox Church, built between 1270 and 1280, is the oldest monument in the town, which today has a population of 33,488 and is growing with the addition of new industries in the neighbourhood.

Bistriţa, which is first mentioned in documents of the twelfth century, when settlers from Germany were brought there, is another town where Saxon interests were paramount; so much so that in 1713 the Romanian population was expelled by order of the Saxon magistrates, but they later returned.

The Bîrgău (or Borgo) Pass, where Count Dracula's carriage was to await Jonathan Harker, is just over fifty miles from Bistriţa. Bram Stoker was accurate in making his hero journey through a 'bewildering mass of fruit blossom – apple, plum, pear, cherry', because Bistriţa was then, as now, a fruit-growing region, but he over-dramatized the landscape with 'an endless perspective of jagged rock and pointed crags' as the coach approached the pass.

The Bîrgău Mountains, nearly 3,700 feet high, are bleak in winter, with the snow, three feet deep at times, lasting from late October or November until mid-May. Deer, Carpathian stag, wolves, wild boars and bears are found in the vicinity. When I was in Bistriţa there was talk of an hotel with 140 beds being built in the pass at a height of 3,600 feet for lovers of natural beauty and skiiers. About 800 yards from the site of the proposed hotel there are the remains of a castle. Efforts have been made to attribute this castle to the historic Dracula but without success.

The road through the pass goes on to Vatra Dornei, a spa and health resort at a height of 2,400 feet surrounded by forest-clad mountains, and to Moldavia with its painted monasteries.

When Jonathan Harker left the 'Golden Crown' hotel the landlord's wife, urging him to delay, said 'It is the eve of St George's Day. Do you know that tonight, when the clock strikes midnight, all the evil things in the world will have full sway?' All is not evil now on St George's Day (23 April). Professor Misiuga, a folklorist, recalled a custom confined to the Bîrgău Valley in which, on St George's Day, unmarried girls jump over a big fire made by local lads. Only one attempt is allowed. If a girl succeeds in jumping over the fire she will get married that year; if not, she must wait for another year.

In another valley, Siului, a turf measuring thirty centimetres by thirty, with a piece of willow in it, is placed on the gatepost of a house where an unmarried girl lives on the eve of St George's Day as an expression of the hope that she will get married that year.

Another marriage custom confined to the Bîrgău Valley and to the period of fasting before Christmas and Easter concerns oxen, which often feature in Romanian folklore. As midnight approaches an unmarried girl will tie a red scarf to the head of an ox. If the ox makes a mooing sound at midnight she will get married that year; if not she must wait another year.

In the village of Joseni, which has 2,000 inhabitants, the ancient tradition known as 'the road tying' is still perpetuated when a wedding is held. Lads who are called 'the inviters' (they go from door to door, accompanied by gipsy musicians, inviting people to the wedding) put a chain between two posts after which one of them, dressed as a bear, starts dancing in the road.

The driver of a car or lorry has to pay before being allowed to continue his journey. The money is not given to the bridegroom but is spent by the revellers. The bearskin used in this ceremony is inherited, said Professor Misiuga. In Romania there is a saying, 'Even the bear dances for money', which is supposed to originate from this custom.

Professor Misiuga considers that the most beautiful custom in Bistriţa-Năsăud is that of *Împănatul Bouloi* or 'the decoration of the oxen' carried out in the little village of Chintelnic, which has a population of only 200. The ceremony, which probably has Indian origins long in the past, is celebrated every year in the second Sunday in June.

After strolling round the village on the Saturday night with the two most beautiful oxen, groups of young and old go to a hill where there are fruit trees and here the ceremony of *Împănatul Bouloi* takes place in secret. Horsemen make garlands of flowers for their mounts, ten youngsters arrange to decorate dogs with flowers, and a larger group pick wild broad beans for the adornment of six youths known as *mositei* who wear masks and helmets made from the bark of the lime tree or the wild cherry. Yet another group pick wild peonies from which they make a garland in four circles which is eventually placed on the horns of one of the oxen. While daylight lasts the *mositei* hunt squirrels, snakes and crows; these are tied to sticks.

A fire is kindled and the night spent in drinking and telling stories. Sleep is forbidden. In the morning the animals and the *mositei* are decorated and at ten o'clock, on the sounding of a trumpet, the procession starts towards the village, accompanied by gipsy musicians. Only one ox has a garland round its horns; the other animal is held in reserve. In the village the procession is awaited by women dressed in their best clothes. Their object is to touch the oxen, but these are carefully garded by the *mositei* with their sticks and by the ten decorated dogs. If a woman manages to put her hand on the oxen the lads are exposed to laughter and scorn and the leadership of the ceremony is taken over by the women, but the *mositei* do not take any chances. They carry vessels of black paint which is thrown over women who get too close. The procession stops in front of each house in the village to allow the owner of it to pour water over the garlands, the group saying ' Long live the owner of this house ', who responds by offering plum brandy, wine and money which goes to pay the musicians.

Professor Misiuga said that in nineteen years of research into folk culture he has not heard of this ceremony being held in any other part of Romania. The procession signifies the dignity and authority of the lads of the village.

This custom of the decoration of the oxen may, as Professor Misiuga suggests, have originated in India, and it is practised in one particular locality, but the *pluguşorul* custom, in which oxen are also involved, had its origin in Romania and is performed over a wide area. *Pluguşorul* (the plough) involves a plough drawn by oxen and a small bottomless barrel covered with skin; by pulling a tuft of hair which passes through the middle of the cover a low sound imitating the roaring of a bull is produced. *Pluguşorul* is accompanied by an oration of thanksgiving for the gifts received for Christmas or during carolling, and in large areas is held on New Year's Eve or New Year's Day, but, as Dr Dumitru Pop has pointed out in a pamphlet, *Pluguşorul in Transilvania,* the ceremony in Transylvania is performed at another date and ' the text is sometimes even included in the wreath oration of the fertility rites during the harvest festival '.

As befits an economy which throughout the centuries has been predominantly agricultural and only now is becoming industrialized, country girls from their mid-teens onwards saw marriage as their destiny and preferably to someone from their own locality; there is still strong prejudice against marriage to a foreigner. Many of the folk beliefs, therefore, are concerned with portents of marriage, and a number which were in vogue ninety years ago are given by Mrs Gerard in *The Land Beyond the Forest.* It is tempting to assume that some, at least, date back to the Impaler's time.

She says that the girl whose thoughts are turned towards love and matrimony has many approved methods of testing her fate on the New Year's night. First of all, she may, by cracking her finger-joints, accurately ascertain the number of her admirers; also, a fresh-laid egg broken into a glass of water will give much clue to the events in store for her by the shape it assumes; and a swine's bristle stuck in a straw and thrown on the heated hearthstone is reliable as a talisman which disperses love or jealousy. To form a conjecture as to the figure and build of her future husband, she is recommended to throw an armful of firewood as far as she can backwards over her shoulder : the piece which has gone farthest will be the image of her intended, according as the stick happens to be long or short, broad or slender, straight or crooked.

Another such game is to place on the table a row of earthen pots upside down. Under each of these is concealed something different – as corn, salt, wool, coals, or money – and the girl is desired to make her choice; thus money stands for a rich husband, and wool for an old one; corn signifies an agriculturalist, and salt connubial happiness, but coals are prophetic of misfortune.

If these general indications do not suffice, and the maiden desires to see the reflection of her bridegroom's face in the water, she has only to step naked at midnight into the nearest lake or river; or if she not unnaturally shrinks from this chilly ordeal, let her, says Mrs Gerard, take her stand on the more congenial dunghill, with a piece of Christmas cake in her mouth, and, as the clock strikes twelve, listen attentively for the first sound of a dog's bark which reaches her ear. From whichever side it proceeds will also come the expected suitor.

Legends abound in the villages around Bistriţa. One, related to me by Dr Vasile Drăguţ in Bucharest, concerns the bas relief of a sow in the village of Iuda. The local legend is that the sow, when rooting in the earth, discovered a treasure from which the church there was built. Quite possibly there is some basis of truth in this legend, unlike that of the pasha and his elephant near Sighişoara. In a land which has been swept by hordes of invaders from the earliest times, what is more natural than that some rich landowner should bury his plate for safety before leaving with his family for the protection of a neighbouring fortress but never returning, and that centuries later the treasure should be discovered during building operations or, as here, by the rooting of a sow?

I was sorry that time did not permit me to visit at Taușoare the deepest caves in Romania, 1,200 feet deep, with two underground streams, but I was fortunate to be able to inspect at the village of Livezile, in apple-tree country a few miles from Bistrița, the treasures of Ion Rusu, a private collector. With an air of justifiable pride Mr Rusu produces for inspection such items as a meteorite, a Stradivarius violin, clocks, swords, ceramics, barometers, clothes and farm implements from former times, icons painted on glass and old photographs. Since the end of the war he has collected 5,000 objects and hopes to double this number. The Romanians take great pride in their ethnographic museums, carefully catalogued and arranged, and I found Mr Rusu's devotion to his haphazard collection, which overflows his house and courtyard, most endearing. There are items here which might well form the basis of an exhibition in a cultural exchange with a Western country.

11 *Maramureş and the flying shepherd*

When I arrived in Maramureş it was with the same feeling of delighted surprise that I had experienced during my first visit to a monastery in Moldavia. There, seeing a group of old women entirely in black waddling to rest under the shade of some trees, I asked my guide 'Who on earth are they?'

'Only peasants' was the reply, but to me they seemed so extraordinary, as if they had stepped out of a Grimm's fairy tale, that I made a discreet circuit of them as they sat on the grass, shapeless in their garments, with work-worn hands and ancient wizened faces. A Western child would have regarded them as a coven of witches. As I travelled to the five painted monasteries in Bukovina, in northern Moldavia, Voronteţ (a miracle in blue built by Stephen the Great in 1488), Humor, Suceviţa, Arbore and Moldoviţa, groups of women dressed in the costumes of the region, and not in black as at Suceava, became familiar sights. They were worshippers, not spectators. It was then I realized that folk costumes were not reserved for festivals but were articles of daily attire.

In Maramureş, a region of Romania that was never occupied by the Romans, the impact of colour in dress was greater, and men and women wore their national dress in the streets of towns – men and boys with a 'clop' on top of their heads (a straw hat with a narrow brim, adorned with hundreds of beads), the women with aprons containing broad horizontal stripes, mostly red or orange. Men and women wore sheepskin jackets without sleeves, embroidered shirts and pointed shoes *(opinci)* tied to the feet by leather straps which go up to the knee.

At Sighetu Marmaţiei, the most northern town in Romania

and also the main economic and cultural centre of Maramureş, I was only one mile from the Soviet border. The road was muddy after recent snow, followed by a thaw, and I gathered from talks with officials that before the region can be fully developed for tourists the existing roads will have to be improved. While the economic need for this is understood, it raises the old problem, for which there is no real answer, of maintaining a balance between the needs of tourism and retaining an unspoiled way of life. The extreme north and south of Romania have most to offer the discriminating traveller, in my opinion – the great spread of the Danube Delta, a wonderland of nature, in the south and Maramureş and the painted monasteries of Moldavia in the north.

Maramureş is the country of wooden cathedrals with slender spires soaring upwards. The arrangement of these wooden churches is singularly uncomplicated, containing the three main rooms, the ante-nave, the nave and the altar laid lengthwise, but the spire, with the open-work balcony of the bell space, and its pyramidal roof, topped by a long arrow, is the most distinctive feature of these buildings. Maramureş is also the country of great carved gates and of chiselled window and door frames. The spiral (a symbol of the soaring aspiration to an ideal) and the sun (a symbol for light and plenty) are the most frequently recurring motifs in the decoration of houses and wooden churches.

Maramureş may give the impression of being a sylvan paradise, but it is, in fact, an old mining settlement. Gold, silver, copper and lead have been mined there since ancient times. One of these mining villages, Cavnic, celebrated its 600th anniversary in August 1974. Forestry is also one of the major industries, and increasing attention is being given to the production of textiles, of which one of the centres is Sighetu Marmaţiei.

We drove past coloured houses to the village of Bogdan Vodă, formerly known as Cuhea. The village was renamed in honour of *Voivode* Bogdan, one of the founders of the Moldavian feudal state, who came from here. In fact, archeologists discovered in the village the stone foundation of a dwelling surrounded by a courtyard where spears, arrow heads, spurs and other objects were found, and the foundations of a stone church dating to the beginning of the fourteenth century.

A document issued by King Louis I of Hungary on 2 February 1365 states that Bogdan and his sons 'passed over in secret' from Maramureş to Moldavia. Professor Giurescu in his history of Transylvania considers that a large part of the Romanians in Maramureş crossed the Carpathians and settled definitely in the new country to the east of the mountains. 'Here, on the borders of Galicia, ie in the region of Bukovina, they found an ancient Romanian population, mentioned in 1164 in the Byzantine chronicle of Nicetas Choniates. It was this ancient Romanian population, which had reached an appreciable level of social and economic development – as proved by its numerous market towns – which formed the basis of the Moldavian state.'

Bogdan was described as a 'notorious infidel' by the Hungarian chancellery because of his refusal to abandon the Orthodox faith for Roman Catholicism. Another reason for his departure to Moldavia was his opposition to the growing tendency of the Magyar feudal kingdom to interfere in the age-old life and social organization of Maramureş.

I had come to Bogdan Vodă in preference to visiting Săpînţa, which has the unusual distinction of having what is probably the only cheerful cemetery in the world. This cemetery has more than 250 crosses adorned by the artist Ion Stan Pătras with sculptures, paintings and drawings in vivid colours depicting in humorous fashion the foibles and virtues of the departed. Time did not permit a visit to both places, however, and I felt, rightly as it turned out, that a couple of hours spent in a cottage could teach me more about the way of life of the people than a conventional round of tourist attractions.

My host at Bogdan Vodă was Mr Vasile Deac, aged forty-six, the deputy-mayor. He explained that there were 3,000 people in the village, which was first documented in 1340. His wife was a midwife *(moaşa)*. Most of the people there worked at animal breeding, fruit farming and forestry. Mr Deac was anxious to show me the interior of the wooden church, built in 1722 and one of the most noted in the district, but it was closed and I had to be satisfied with his description of the carved wood chandelier and the paintings, the older ones like miniatures and the more recent ones in the spirit of late baroque.

In the house we were escorted to the guest room which was, in fact, seldom used ('never used', I was told at the time, and from its spotless condition I could believe this). Here there were wall carpets, ceramics, icons, embroidered towels which had not been touched by hand, and spoons and forks carved from wood. In the same room the parents kept their daughter's dowry of hand-made decorated blankets, pillows and wall carpets. In the 1880s Mrs Gerard wrote that 'the preparation of the trousseau, involving as it does much spinning, weaving and embroidering, in order to get the requisite number of shirts, towels, pillowslips, etc, considered indispensable often keeps the girl and her family employed for years beforehand', and this is obviously still true today.

In the kitchen-living-room the elder daughter Cornelia, aged fourteen, was making a wall carpet on a loom, supervised by her mother. At the same time she watched an old American musical comedy flickering dimly on a TV screen, but this was switched off on our entry. The loom still plays a big part in Romanian peasant life, despite the availability of clothing and articles of household use in the shops. A century or so ago the looms were very primitive – a frame of coarse logs, held together by plugs, as Boner observed – but on it the wife weaved the thick woollen stuff in which her husband was clothed.

The sandals he has on he made himself, being simply a piece of thick leather, the ends and sides lapped over round the foot, and held fast by a thong of great length that is wound round the leg. The strip of stuff in which the foot is swathed before putting on the sandal is also a bit of homespun shirt or jacket, so that the whole man is encased in home produce and home manufacture. On his head he wears a cap made of the skin of one of his own sheep or lambs.

A wife would make many articles of her own clothing, accord-ing to Boner, on

that incomprehensible primitive machine which they call a loom
and she even makes the dyes given to the wool; but these are all
produced from vegetable substances. For one colour a certain plant
was sought that grew among the rocks; for bright yellow the buds
of willows were taken, and so on till each hue and every gradation
wanted had been obtained.

The looms of today are, of course, much more sophisticated,
although essentially simple in design, and it is no longer necessary
to make dyes from plants, but the widespread use of the loom in
present times is but another indication of the perpetuation of a
centuries-old pattern in peasant life.

While Cornelia was busy on her loom a large round loaf of
bread and smoked pork fat was placed on the table and we were
offered home-made *horincă,* a doubly-distilled plum brandy
which sets the blood coursing through the veins. Our host, a
peasant (and this is a proud term in modern Romania – how
often have I been told by a professor that 'my father, or grandfather, was a peasant') made a speech in which he wished us
health, success, and expressed his satisfaction at our visit. He
called in his eighty-two-year-old father who crossed himself, put
his hands together, and prayed to God to give us health, happiness, luck and success also for our sons, whom he called 'the
little roosters'. When the interpreter, at my suggestion, asked if
the same success was meant for our daughters the old man
repeated the prayer for 'the little roosters', thus indicating, I
was told, the importance placed on boys.

Our host and his father, as a mark of respect for their guests,
did not eat with us. We were served with smoked pork fat eaten
with onions, *plăcinta,* a thick pancake fried in sunflower oil,
containing cheese or marmalade and fried cabbage, the result
being something between a cake and bread, sweet cheese mixed
with cream that has been slightly soured, and the favourite
national dish of *mămăligă,* yellow in colour, made from maize
powder mixed with water and salt and stirred until it became
thick. In some villages it often replaces bread.

Pleasantly warmed by this excellent meal and the flowing
horincă, I asked our host if there was still belief in ghosts in the

village. He started hesitatingly (I noticed time and again that Romanians, in this scientific age, are afraid of being thought superstitious, as if this were a slur, while at the same time stressing the importance of preserving folk beliefs), but as he warmed to his task his eyes flashed and he spoke with fervour.

Folk beliefs were not now widely held, Mr Deac said, but belief in ghosts still existed, although you could only hear about them from old people.

One such tale was told by Maria Buftea, who died in 1974 at the age of ninety-three. When she was eighteen she called her sister, who was a midwife, to a woman who was about to have a baby. As her sister did not come at once she set out alone on the return journey. She had the impression that she was being followed by a man, who later took the shape of a horse. As soon as she reached the gate of her house she heard the horse neighing, but the people who came out at her insistence did not see the horse nor did her sister, the midwife, on her journey. The horse, she was convinced, was a *strigoi*, and she was ill for seven weeks as a result of this experience.

Mr Deac said that his mother, who died in 1971 aged eighty-two, told him that about sixty years ago a man named Dumitru and his wife from that village went haymaking together. Dumitru absented himself, and presently his wife, who was on top of the haystack, was attacked by a dog which jumped at her, biting her apron. While calling her husband she defended herself vigorously with the rake, hitting the dog until it ran away. The woman jumped off the haystack and again shouted for her husband. After a while he appeared, looking very unhappy. She then noticed that her husband had a piece of her apron in his teeth and blood marks on his head in the place where she had hit the dog. The woman then knew that her husband was the dog which had attacked her and accused him of this. He admitted it and asked her not to tell anyone. After this Dumitru would disappear for nights at a time and his wife knew that he was then roaming around as a dog.

It seemed strange to me that a woman would be content to stay married under such circumstances. Mr Deac, in reply to this, said that villagers had warned the woman before marriage that her intended was a *strigoi*, but she had not believed them until the incident on the haystack. Despite this they stayed together until his death.

Mr Deac said he had heard from an old woman that a descendant of Dumitru had given birth to two dogs which were killed on the spot. I related this story to Dr Bărbulescu on my return to Bucharest. He said that the story about the dog biting an apron or dress and a man being seen afterwards with a piece of the missing material in his teeth started in Maramureş and was known as far south as Sibiu.

Eight years or so ago Dr Bărbulescu heard in Bucharest that a woman had given birth to two dogs. His prompt investigation proved that the 'dogs' were small twins, described by someone who had seen them as 'like little puppies'. Possibly this is the explanation for what was said to have happened at Bogdan Vodă.

To return to the village and an interesting folk custom that still takes place there. On New Year's Eve and on 6 January some girls break the ice on the river Iza to place sweet basil in the chilly water. If the frozen flowers were still there before sunrise it meant that they would be married to good husbands in the coming year. If a girl's flowers had disappeared it meant that the husband-to-be had died and she would never marry. Occasionally the flowers would be taken by a village lad whose attentions to the girl had been discouraged by her parents. It was possible that after the disappearance of the flowers the boy would be accepted as a second choice or, if that did not happen, the young couple might run away together and then get her parents' permission to marry.

Mr Deac told the story of his grandfather's brother who was employed by a rich man as a shepherd. During the winter his sheep were kept in the open. The young shepherd was in love with a girl who lived some distance away, but the match was opposed by his parents, although the girl's parents were in favour of it, as she was poor. They therefore used magic to bring him to her. They did this by making the shape of a body on the ground with two glowing stakes heated in the fire on either side. Then they boiled special water called *apa Sîmbetei* (the water of Saturday) and the water of Friday, *apa Vinerei,* until it started evaporating. While the water was boiling they uttered incantations which resulted in the shepherd's being raised 'high in the air by unknown powers and brought flying to the girl's place'. But because the iron was too hot and the water boiled too much the shepherd was carried too high and was ill for three days, thus being unable to return to his sheepfold. The shepherd later married the girl despite the opposition of his parents, because her parents were regarded as 'ghosts' and as such avoided by other people. Descendants of this family still live in the village, Mr Deac said.

This strange story of a man being propelled through the air has some parallels in one told by Uri Geller, the young Israeli whose powers of bending metal have perplexed scientists, in his autobiography *Uri Geller: My Story.* It concerns Geller himself, who admits that 'There is no way I can tell this story without having it sound like science fiction', adding 'The main problem is the physical impossibility of what happened in terms of ordinary time and distance, and the laws of physics as we know them.'

On 9 November 1973 Uri Geller was returning to his apartment in Manhattan.

I clearly remember approaching the canopy of the building right next door to ours. I remember almost reaching that canopy. Then I remember having the feeling that I was running backwards for a couple of steps. I don't know whether I really did or not, but that was the feeling. Then I had the feeling that I was being sucked upward. There was no sensation in my body. I closed my eyes and, I think, opened them almost immediately. When I did, I felt myself being propelled in the air a foot or so away from a porch screen, over the top of a rhododendron bush, about to crash through the screen at a point eight or ten feet off the ground. To prepare for the impact, I turned my left shoulder toward the screen and put my hands out in front of me. I crashed through the screen and landed on a circular glass-top table. . . .

Uri Geller had arrived at the home of his friend Dr Andrida Puharich in Ossining, thirty-six miles from Manhattan. Geller asks 'What kind of transformation or transportation did my body undergo? Was I really torn up molecule by molecule? Was I pushed through a dimension, teleported by a ray or by a spacecraft? What happened? I don't know.'

Powers of levitation, but not of instant transportation over considerable distances, were ascribed to the physical medium D. D. Home in the last century, but we must avoid being drawn into these tempting bypaths of speculation and return to Bogdan Vodă.

I was thinking over the events of the day when we returned to Baia Mare, crossing Mount Gutîi, over 4,000 feet high, the road thick with fallen leaves and the trees still snow-covered. Earlier I had met Professor Ion Chiş Ster, head of the Folklore Course at the High School, who said that several years ago he had talked to a man of eighty-two who told him that fifty years ago he was driving home his cows when the bladder of the one with the best yield swelled to double its size and the animal dropped dead. The old man attributed this to witchcraft.

I was sorry to leave Maramureş. It is a district with less than half a million people, but among this small population 15,000 amateurs take an active part in the arts. Despite increasing industrialization (at Baia Mare, for instance, there is a great chemical-metallurgical combine and there are also enterprises for the extraction of mineral ores) the countryside is unspoiled. The exploitation (in the nice sense of the word) of the district's natural resources has resulted in better housing and an improvement in the standard of living. Between 1960 and 1974 the State has constructed 20,000 apartments and another 26,000 have been built privately.

There was much that I still wanted to see. If I had been able to visit the district at the end of the following month (April) I could have seen at Giuleşti the old folklore festival called *Tînjaua* (*tînja* is a pole with a forked end attached to the shaft) held to honour the peasant who was the first to begin the spring ploughing. Or at nearby Hărniceşti I could have inspected in the church the three valuable icons painted on wood which have been exhibited at London, Paris and Stuttgart. If time permitted when I was at Bogdan Vodă I could have gone on to the village of Moisei in that vicinity where, in 1944, German troops shot thirty guerilla fighters gathered in a house after which they robbed and set fire to the whole commune. Now there is a new village and the memory of the twenty-nine victims (one of the guerilla fighters survived) is kept alive by a large sculpture, the work of Gheza Vida, which consists of twelve stylized silhouettes standing around an oval stone table. These sights, and many more, await my next visit.

Every traveller brings back from a country certain memories which remain after others have been mostly forgotten. One from an earlier visit to Romania concerns a visit to the Danube Delta, where I stayed in a fisherman's cottage at Murighiol (the Turkish word for violet lake), ate freshly-caught fish under a trellis over which a vine trailed, and spent hours being rowed through channels among reeds and in watching birds, including pelicans. Another is of standing on the ramparts of Dracula's Castle while ravens circled overhead under a blazing blue sky and thinking of the sweating boyars who had been forced by the Impaler to rebuild his mountain refuge. A third is of my stay at Bogdan Vodă. Romanians, I have noticed, have a gift for dramatic narrative, and a sense of the past, which is understandable in a country so steeped in history. The beliefs of the old are not a subject for mirth, and although ghosts and werewolves may not cause the fear they once evoked, they still have their place in the living folklore of the countryside as well as in the archives of scholars.

12 Voices from the past

In reviewing three books for children on folk themes in *The Times Literary Supplement* on 1 October 1976 Judith Vidal Hall said that 'Folktale is frequently the only tangible legacy of a culture now gone or at least so changed as to be scarcely recognizable for what it was. . . .', thereby putting into words something that had been at the back of my mind since I started research for this book. The tales I have related here come down as voices from the past, voices, alas, that will all too soon be silenced. It will have been noticed that all my informants were old and, in some instances, very old, or that the stories given to me at second-hand related to the past. As any experienced investigator in psychical research knows, a tale from the past, or something experienced in the past, tends to become personalized, so that in time the person who relates the incident claims that it happened to him. But in making allowance for this, patterns may be discerned, such as in the persisting story of the man changed into a dog or wolf who is found, after resuming human form, to have a portion of cloth from his wife's dress or apron in his teeth. The fact that I have come across such a story in different parts of Transylvania indicates that it is a genuine folk belief.

The problem, of course, is how these folk beliefs should be interpreted. There is, quite obviously, a continuing belief in witchcraft among some old people in country districts in Romania just as there is in England and in other Western countries. Time and again I was told that 'Romanian people are not superstitious', but we have evidence from writers in the past century such as Emily Gerard that they were then very

superstitious, and I believe that some, at least, of these super-
stitions persist to the present day, just as they do in other
countries. In some villages the *popa* assured me that his people
were not superstitious and he could not put me in touch with an
old person who had first-hand knowledge of past beliefs, but I
have little doubt that if I had been able to stay there long
enough the information I wanted would have come to light.

Some stories may be greeted with a smile, such as that of the
witch riding the dragon, and, despite widespread belief in many
countries that men and women can take the form of animals and
then resume human shape, there is no scientific evidence that
anything like this actually happens. Members of certain secret
cults in Africa wear the skins of leopards or other animals during
the commission of their crimes, and such a practice can cause
confusion as to whether the killing was carried out by a man or
a beast of prey. There have not been such secret societies in
Transylvania, however, and most accounts of werewolves concern
attacks on sheep or cattle and the occasional human being. It is
extraordinarily interesting that there is still a lingering belief in
werewolves among the old in Transylvania.

There is also a lingering belief in ghosts in Transylvania :
living people who, in different places, may be described as
ghosts or witches, and there are more sinister ghosts who leave
the grave. I do not believe that a body can leave the grave, and
subscribe to the scepticism of the Romanian scholars on this
point, but there is, in my opinion, plenty of evidence that some
people in good bodily and mental health do see apparitions. I
did not come across a Romanian scholar who conceded that this
was so, however, and in a book such as this I want to reflect
Romanian opinion and not impose my own.

Until a certain age, I was told, modern youngsters in Romania
tend to shy away from old traditions, but when they marry they
often revert to accepting some old beliefs and these are enriched
when they meet people from other parts of the country who have
settled in town. I can remember discussing this point of the
preservation of old beliefs with a panel of scholars at Cluj
University during one of my early visits to Transylvania, and

remember vividly their insistence that such beliefs can never be extinguished but find new expression in folk art and in the sculpture of an artist of the stature of Constantin Brăncuşi, who was born in Romania.

There is little doubt that folk traditions will be maintained in Romania. The encouragement of folk traditions in all forms of the arts was one of the themes stressed at the first national congress on Specialist Education and Culture held in Bucharest in May 1976 and attended by a thousand delegates. The avoidance of what was described to me as 'spiritual pollution' was another theme of the congress and I was given to understand that Bram Stoker's *Dracula* would come into this category.

This has been a book about Romanian folk beliefs, but it should not be overlooked that the Hungarian and German elements of the population have their own folk beliefs and customs. For instance, in driving from Tîrgu Mureş, of which the guide book says that 'the history of the settlement is full of dramatic events, unrest and ferocious epidemics', to Sighişoara we passed through villages where the houses, and in particular the gates, were decorated for Easter (that of the Western Church) in a most elaborate way with fir branches, ribbons, rosettes, and red eggs on string. These decorations were placed on the homes of unmarried girls by their admirers. The young men of the village watched over the house on the first night of Easter lest the decorations be stolen to adorn other houses and the girls looked out from above for the same purpose. Then, on the first day of Easter, the boys threw perfume over the girls, saying that just as flowers needed watering, so did they. On the second day of Easter children joined in the jollity by throwing water and we saw one luckless youth shaking the moisture from him amid laughing onlookers. This, I was told, was not a Romanian custom.

Transylvania has been fortunately placed for the preservation of folk beliefs. In the past century, mainly owing to poor communications, it was an odd corner of Europe, attracting few travellers, and the villagers did not come under Western influences. Now, owing to the political climate, large sections of the population have not travelled in the West nor met Western visitors in the mountain villages. But with increasing industrialization, the growth of tourism and the concentration of the population in the larger centres, a way of life is changing rapidly, and a television set takes the place of tales told round the hearth.

The days when Romania was a scarcely visited part of Europe have gone for ever, although, as I have pointed out, little has changed in the lives of old people in isolated villages or in their beliefs. There were more than fifteen million foreign tourists between 1971 and 1975. A great many went to the resorts on the Black Sea, to Bucharest, and to the well developed mountain resorts, but there are also cultural holidays, and itineraries are arranged which help tourists to get acquainted with folklore. My own feeling is that the more mountain resorts are developed the better as they provide access by walking or by car to villages of the type I have described. You can get to know a country only by rambling through it and by returning to it again and again, but organized tours are necessary, particularly when there are difficulties of language and accommodation.

It is still possible to wander through Transylvania, and other parts of Romania, and come quite by chance on folk customs 'in action' in a way that is no longer possible in many Western countries. If I had been able to sit down for a day with Professor Alexandru Misiuga in Bistriţa I could have filled notebook after notebook with accounts of folk customs still observed in the vicinity of the Bîrgău Pass where Bram Stoker placed Dracula's Castle. In a sense, Stoker chose better than he knew because this is a district rich in folk beliefs.

The 'voices from the past' in the heading of this chapter are those captured by the researchers on tape in their excursions into the field. Although there are chairs of folklore in the universities in Romania, there are only ten, or at the most fifteen, scientific researchers of note. The work they are doing is, in my opinion, invaluable. In his foreword to the reprinted *Bloodstoppers and Bearwalkers,* the distinguished American folklorist, Professor Richard M. Dorson, says that

Today, two decades after the publication of *Bloodstoppers and Bearwalkers,* the public and the scholarly world increasingly recognize that folklore comes from the spoken word, and that such oral folklore is one of the chief avenues into the lives and minds of anonymous Americans. The red man, the black man, the immigrant, the labourer in the woods, mines and factories, the man in the street, and the woman in the nursery may have left us little or nothing in the way of written records but they have bequeathed us absorbing verbal traditions of their experiences and concerns.

This observation can also apply to the accounts collected by Romanian researchers.

The themes of some folk beliefs, such as that of the werewolf or some other were-animal, span the globe. Professor Dorson gives instances of belief in the *loup-garou* among French Canadians, and these derive ultimately from France. Some Romanian folk beliefs contain elements from other cultures but others are quite distinctive and must be preserved before they disappear. So, when the researcher goes into the field with his tape recorder, he obtains from the villagers tales of old Transylvania, Moldavia and Wallachia relating to a way of life that is fast vanishing. No one who has been, as I have, in the cottages of old people can fail to be moved by the conviction with which these stories are related. They are the products of an economy tied to crops and flocks. Now, with industrial centres in Romania ringed by the familiar high-rise flats, a new economy is in evidence. The changed way of life of so many of the people will be poorer without the enrichment of folk beliefs held over many centuries. In a strange sort of way, the folk tales about the historical Dracula are part of this legacy.

Select Bibliography

I have confined this selection of books to those in English and, as I have indicated, there is no reliable volume in English about Romanian folklore. There is, however, *Zeitschrift Für Balkanologie* in German by Dr Dumitru Pop with C. Sǎteanu (Munich, 1975) which deals with Romanian folklore in a European context. Dr Corneliu Bǎrbulescu has been compiling a book of case histories from his Institute and this, I gather, may be published also in French. Dr Pavelescu's works on folklore, folk medicine and magical beliefs in the mountains would, I am certain, attract much interest if published in English.

Among books on the Dracula cult the following are recommended:

Farson, Daniel, *The man who wrote Dracula, a biography of Bram Stoker* (London, 1975).

Florescu, Radu, and McNally, Raymond T., *In Search of Dracula* (New York, 1973).

Florescu, Radu, and McNally, Raymond T., *Dracula, a Biography* (London, 1974). This book is particularly recommended for the bibliography and for the notes.

Ludlam, Harry, *A Biography of Dracula, The Life Story of Bram Stoker* (London, 1962).

Wolf, Leonard, *The Annotated Dracula*. With introduction, notes and bibliography (London, 1976).

Ronay, Gabriel, *The Dracula Myth* (London, 1972).

Among books on werewolves the best is probably *The Werewolf*, by Montague Summers, Kegan Paul (London, 1933, and New York, 1966). The author, although learned, is credulous, but his book does give an indication of the extent of the cult in past ages.

Other books:

Beza, Marcu, *Paganism in Roumanian Folklore* (London, 1928).

Boner, Charles, *Transylvania: Its Products and Its People* (London, 1865).

Briggs, K. M., *A Dictionary of British Folk Tales* (London, 1971).

Dorson, Richard M., *Folktales Told Around the World* (Chicago, 1975).

Frazer, James, *The Golden Bough* (London, 1890).

Gaster, Moses, *Children's Stories From Roumanian Legends and Fairy Tales* (London, 1923).

——, *Rumanian Bird and Beast Stories* (London, 1915).

Gerard, Emily, *The Land Beyond the Forest* (London and Edinburgh, 1888).

Giurescu, Constantin C., *Transylvania in the History of Romania* (London, undated).

Gould, George M. and Pyle, Walter L., *Anomalies and Curiosities of Medicine* (London, 1897).

Neagoe, Peter, *Easter Sun* (London, 1934).

Seton-Watson, R. W., *The Rise of Nationality in the Balkans* (London, 1917).

——, *A History of the Roumanians from Roman Times to the Completion of Unity* (Cambridge, 1934).

Starkie, Walter, *Raggle-Taggle. Adventures with a Fiddle in Hungary and Rumania* (London, 1933).

Verne, Jules, *The Castle of the Carpathians* (London, 1893).

I should also mention Dr Ştefan Pascu's *History of Transylvania* (Blaj, 1944), and the more recent *Voievodatul Transilvaniei* (Cluj, 1971).

Walker, Mary Adelaide, *Untrodden Paths in Roumania* (London, 1888).

Index